12th Conference of the European Chapter of the Association for Computational Linguistics 2009 (EACL 2009)

Demonstrations

Athens, Greece
3 April 2009

ISBN: 978-1-63266-012-1

Printed from e-media with permission by:

Curran Associates, Inc.
57 Morehouse Lane
Red Hook, NY 12571

CURRAN ASSOCIATES INC.
proceedings
.com

Some format issues inherent in the e-media version may also appear in this print version.

Printed by Curran Associates, Inc. (2014)

Association for Computational Linguistics
209 N. Eighth Street
Stroudsburg, Pennsylvania 18360

Phone: 1-570-476-8006
Fax: 1-570-476-0860

acl@aclweb.org

Additional copies of this publication are available from:

Curran Associates, Inc.
57 Morehouse Lane
Red Hook, NY 12571 USA
Phone: 845-758-0400
Fax: 845-758-2634
Email: curran@proceedings.com
Web: www.proceedings.com

EACL 2009

Proceedings of the Demonstrations Session

3 April 2009
Megaron Athens International Conference Centre
Athens, Greece

Preface

The short papers reproduced here describe implemented systems that were presented at the demo session of EACL-2009 in Athens, March 30 - April 3, 2009.

Upon the call for demos, a total of 33 papers were submitted. Each submission was reviewed by at least two members of the programme committee. Based on these reviews, 17 submissions were accepted for presentation at the demo session and publication in the conference proceedings.

I would like to thank the general chairs and the local organisers, without whom it would have been impossible to put together such a strong demo programme. In particular, I would like to thank the members of the programme committee for the excellent job they did in reviewing the submissions.

Jörn Kreutel

EACL 2009 Demonstration Chair

Program Committee

Program Chair:

Jörn Kreutel, Semantic Edge (Germany)

Program Committee Members:

Ulrich Callmeier, Acrolinx GmbH (Germany)
Berry Claus, Saarland University (Germany)
Antske Fokkens, Saarland University (Germany)
Mary Ellen Foster, Technical University of Munich (Germany)
Chris Geib, University of Edinburgh (UK)
Manuel Giuliani, Technical University of Munich (Germany)
David Horowitz, University of Trento (Italy)
Amy Isard, University of Edinburgh (UK)
Remco Loos, Rovira i Virgili University, (Spain)
Titus von der Malsburg, University of Potsdam (Germany)
Colin Matheson, University of Edinburgh (UK)
Bart Mellebeek, Barcelona Media (Spain)
Stefan Müller, Free University of Berlin (Germany)
Melanie Siegel, Acrolinx GmbH (Germany)
Wojciech Skut, Google Inc. (USA)

Table of Contents

Frolog: an accommodating text-adventure game

Luciana Benotti
TALARIS Team - LORIA (Université Henri Poincaré, INRIA)
BP 239, 54506 Vandoeuvre-lès-Nancy, France
Luciana.Benotti@loria.fr

Abstract

Frolog is a text-adventure game whose goal is to serve as a laboratory for testing pragmatic theories of accommodation. To this end, rather than implementing ad-hoc mechanisms for each task that is necessary in such a conversational agent, Frolog integrates recently developed tools from computational linguistics, theorem proving and artificial intelligence planning.

1 Introduction

If we take a dialogue perspective on Lewis' (1979) notion of *accommodation* and assume that the state of a dialogue is changed by the acts performed by the dialogue participants, it is natural to interpret Lewis' broad notion of accommodation as *tacit (or implicit) dialogue acts*. This is the approach adopted by Kreutel and Matheson (2003) who formalize the treatment of tacit dialogue acts in the information state update framework. According to them, accommodation is ruled by the following principle:

Context Accommodation (CA): For any move m *that ocurrs in a given scenario* sc_i*: if assignment of a context-dependent interpretation to* m *in* sc_i *fails, try to accommodate* sc_i *to a new context* sc_{i+1} *in an appropriate way by assuming implicit dialogue acts performed in* m*, and start interpretation of* m *again in* sc_{i+1}.

The authors concentrate on the treatment of implicit acceptance acts but suggest that the CA principle can be seen as a general means of context-dependent interpretation. This principle opens up the question of how to find the appropriate tacit dialogue acts. Finding them is an inference problem that is addressed using special-purpose algorithms in (Thomason et al., 2006), where the authors present a unified architecture for both context-dependent interpretation and context-dependent generation. In Frolog, we investigate how this inference process can be implemented using recent tools from *artificial intelligence planning*.

The resulting framework naturally lends itself to studying the pressing problem for current theories of accommodation called *missing accommodation* (Beaver and Zeevat, 2007). These theories can neither explain *why* accommodation is sometimes easier and sometimes much more difficult, nor *how* cases of missing accommodation relate to clarification subdialogues in conversation. We review what Frolog has to offer to the understanding of accommodation in general and missing accommodation in particular in Section 3. But first, we have to introduce Frolog and describe its components, and we do so in Section 2.

2 The text-adventure game

Text-adventures are computer games that simulate a physical environment which can be manipulated by means of natural language requests. The game provides feedback in the form of natural language descriptions of the game world and of the results of the players' actions.

Frolog is based on a previous text-adventure called FrOz (Koller et al., 2004) and its design is depicted in Figure 1. The architecture is organized in three natural language understanding (NLU) modules and three natural language generation (NLG) modules, and the state of the interaction is represented in two knowledge bases (KBs). The two KBs codify, in Description Logic (Baader et al., 2003), assertions and concepts relevant for a given game scenario. The *game KB* represents the true state of the game world, while the *player KB* keeps track of the player's beliefs about the game world. Frolog's modules are scenario-independent; the player can play different game scenarios by plugging in the different information resources that constitute the scenario.

Frolog uses generic external tools for the most heavy-loaded tasks (depicted in grey in Figure 1);

Proceedings of the EACL 2009 Demonstrations Session, pages 1–4,
Athens, Greece, 3 April 2009.

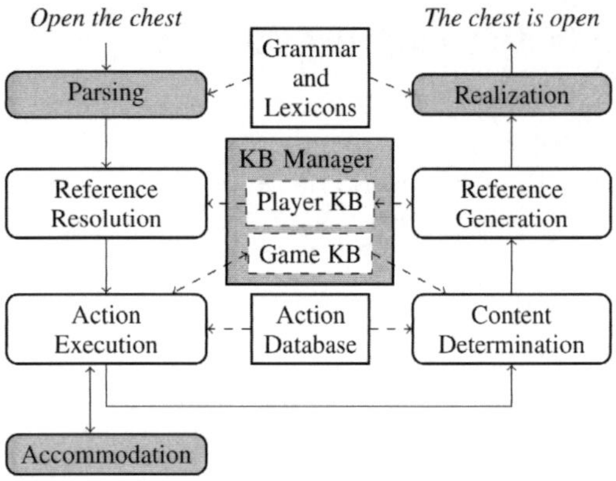

Figure 1: Architecture of Frolog

namely, a generic parser and a generic realizer for parsing and realization, an automated theorem prover for knowledge base management, and artificial intelligence planners for implementing its accommodating capabilities. The rest of the modules (depicted in white) were implemented by us in Prolog and Java. Frolog's interface shows the interaction with the player, the input/output of each module and the content of the KBs.

We now present Frolog's modules in pairs of an NLU module and its NLG counterpart; each pair uses a particular kind of information resource and has analogous input/output.

2.1 Parsing and Realization

The parsing and the realization modules use the same linguistic resources, namely a reversible grammar, a lemma lexicon and a morphological lexicon represented in the XMG grammatical formalism (Crabbé and Duchier, 2004). The XMG grammar used specifies a Tree Adjoining Grammar (TAG) of around 500 trees and integrates a semantic dimension à la (Gardent, 2008). An example of the semantics associated with the player input "open the chest" is depicted in Figure 2.

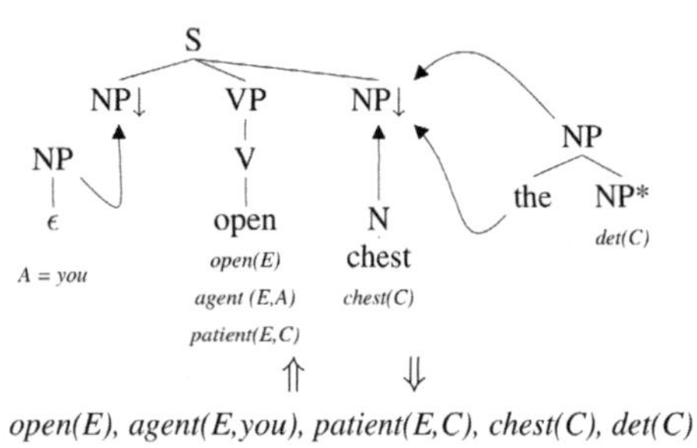

Figure 2: Parsing/realization for "open the chest"

The parsing module performs the syntactic analysis of a command issued by the player, and constructs its semantic representation using the TAG parser Tulipa (Kallmeyer et al., 2008) (illustrated in the Figure 2 by ⇓). The realization module works in the opposite direction, verbalizing the results of the execution of the command from the semantic representation using the TAG surface realizer GenI (Gardent and Kow, 2007) (illustrated in the Figure 2 by ⇑).

2.2 Reference Resolution and Reference Generation

The reference resolution (RR) module is responsible for mapping the semantic representations of definite and indefinite noun phrases and pronouns to individuals in the knowledge bases (illustrated in Figure 3 by ⇓). The reference generation (RG) module performs the inverse task, that is it generates the semantic representation of a noun phrase that uniquely identifies an individual in the knowledge bases (illustrated in the Figure 3 by ⇑). The algorithms used for RR and RG are described in (Koller et al., 2004).

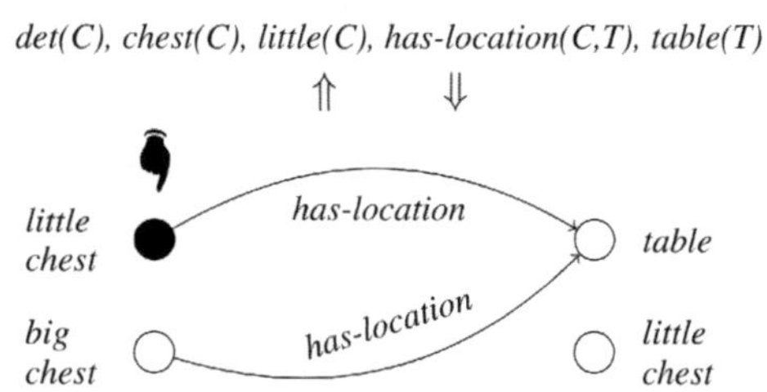

Figure 3: RR/RG for "the little chest on the table"

Frolog uses the theorem prover RACER (Haarslev and Möller, 2001) to query the KBs and perform RR and RG. In order to manage the ambiguity of referring expressions two levels of saliency are considered. The player KB is queried (instead of the game KB) naturally capturing the fact that the player will not refer to individuals he doesn't know about (even if they exist in the game KB). Among the objects that the player already knows, a second level of saliency is modelled employing a simple stack of discourse referents which keeps track of the most recently referred individuals. A new individual gets into the player KB when the player explores the world.

2.3 Action Execution and Content Determination

These two last modules share the last information resource that constitute an scenario, namely, the action database. The action database includes the definitions of the actions that can be executed by the player (such as *take* or *open*). Each action is specified as a STRIPS-like operator (Fikes et al., 1972) detailing its arguments, preconditions and effects as illustrated below. The arguments show the thematic roles of the verb (for instance, the verb open requires a patient and an agent), the preconditions indicate the conditions that the game world must satisfy so that the action can be executed (for instance, in order to open the chest, it has to be accessible, unlocked and closed); the effects determine how the action changes the game world when it is executed (after opening the chest, it will be open).

action: open(E) agent(E,A) patient(E,P)
preconditions: accessible(P), not(locked(P)), closed(P)
effects: opened(P)

Executing a player's command amounts to verifying whether the preconditions of the actions involved by the command hold in the game world and, if they do, changing the game KB according to the effects. After the command is executed, the content determination module constructs the semantic representation of the effects that were applied, updates the player KB with it and passes it to the next module for its verbalization (so that the player knows what changed in the world). For our running example the following modules will verbalize "the chest is open" closing a complete cycle of the system as illustrated in Figure 1.

If a precondition of an action does not hold then Frolog tries to accommodate as we will explain in following section.

3 Accommodation in Frolog

In the previous section we presented the execution of the system when everything "goes well", that is (to come back to the terminology used in Section 1) when the assignment of a context-dependent interpretation to the player's move succeeds. However, during the interaction with Frolog, it often happens that the player issues a command that cannot be directly executed in the current state of the game but needs accommodation or clarification. This is the topic of the next two subsections.

3.1 Tacit acts are inferable and executable: accommodation succeeds

Suppose that the player has just locked the little chest and left its key on the table when she realizes that she forgot to take the sword from it, so she utters "open the chest". If Frolog is in its non-accommodating mode then it answers "the chest is locked" because the precondition *not(locked(P))* does not hold in the game world. In this mode, the interactions with the game can get quite long and repetitive as illustrated below.

Non-accommodating mode	Accommodating mode
P: open the chest	P: open the chest
F: the chest is locked	F: the chest is open
P: unlock it	
F: you don't have the key	
...	

In its accommodating mode, Frolog tries to accommodate the current state sc_i of the game to a new state sc_{i+1} in which the precondition hold, by assuming tacit dialogue acts performed, and starts the interpretation of the command again in sc_{i+1}. That is, the game assumes that "take the key and unlock the chest with it" are tacit acts that are performed when the player says "open the chest".

The inference of such tacit dialogue acts is done using artificial intelligence planners. The planning problems are generated on the fly during a game each time a precondition does not hold; the initial state being the player KB, the goal being the precondition that failed, and the action schemas those actions available in the action database. The size of the plans can be configured, when the length is zero we say that Frolog is in its non-accommodating mode. For detailed discussion of the subtleties involved in the kind of information that has to be used to infer the tacit acts see (Benotti, 2007).

Two planners have been integrated in Frolog (the player can decide which one to use): Blackbox (Kautz and Selman, 1999) which is *fast and deterministic* and PKS (Petrick and Bacchus, 2004) which can reason over *non-deterministic actions*. For detailed discussion and examples including non-deterministic actions see (Benotti, 2008).

3.2 Accommodation fails: clarification starts

Tacit acts are inferred using the information available to the player (the player KB) but their execution is verified with respect to the accurate and complete state of the world (the game KB). So

Frolog distinguishes three ways in which accommodation can fail: there is no plan, there is more than one plan, or there is a plan which is not executable in the game world. For reasons of space we will only illustrate the last case here.

Suppose that the golden key, which was lying on the table, was taken by a thief without the player knowing. As a consequence, the key is on the table in the player KB, but in the game KB the thief has it. In this situation, the player issues the command "Open the chest" and the sequence of tacit acts inferred (given the player beliefs) is "take the key from the table and unlock the chest with it". When trying to execute the tacit acts, the game finds the precondition that does not hold and verbalizes it with "the key is not on the table, you don't know where it is". Such answer can be seen as a clarification request (CR), it has the effect of assigning to the player the responsability of finding the key before trying to open the chest. The same responsability that would be assigned by more commonly used CR that can happen in this scenario, namely "Where is the key?".

In the game, such clarifications vary according to the knowledge that is currently available to the player. If the player knows that the dragon has the key and she can only take it while the dragon is asleep an answer such as "the dragon is not sleeping" is generated in the same fashion.

4 Conclusion and future work

In this paper we have presented a text-adventure game which is an interesting test-bed for experimenting with accommodation. The text-adventure framework makes evident the strong relation between accommodation and clarification (which is not commonly studied), highlighting the importance of investigating accommodation in dialogue and not in isolation.

Our work is in its early stages and can be advanced in many directions. We are particularly interested in modifying the architecture of the system in order to model reference as another action instead of preprocessing references with special-purpose algorithms. In this way we would not only obtain a more elegant architecture, but also be able to investigate the interactions between reference and other kinds of actions, which occur in every-day conversations.

References

F. Baader, D. Calvanese, D. McGuinness, D. Nardi, and P. Patel-Schneider. 2003. *The Description Logic Handbook: Theory, Implementation, and Applications*. Cambridge University Press.

D. Beaver and H. Zeevat. 2007. Accommodation. In *The Oxford Handbook of Linguistic Interfaces*, pages 503–539. Oxford University Press.

L. Benotti. 2007. Incomplete knowledge and tacit action: Enlightened update in a dialogue game. In *Proc. of DECALOG*, pages 17–24.

L. Benotti. 2008. Accommodation through tacit sensing. In *Proc. of LONDIAL*, pages 75–82.

B. Crabbé and D. Duchier. 2004. Metagrammar redux. In *Proc. of CSLP04*.

R. Fikes, P. Hart, and N. Nilsson. 1972. Learning and executing generalized robot plans. *AI*, 3:251–288.

C. Gardent and E. Kow. 2007. A symbolic approach to near-deterministic surface realisation using tree adjoining grammar. In *Proc. of ACL07*.

C. Gardent. 2008. Integrating a unification-based semantics in a large scale lexicalised tree adjoininig grammar for french. In *Proc. of COLING08*.

V. Haarslev and R. Möller. 2001. RACER system description. In *Proc. of IJCAR01*, number 2083 in LNAI, pages 701–705.

L. Kallmeyer, T. Lichte, W. Maier, Y. Parmentier, J. Dellert, and K. Evang. 2008. TuLiPA: Towards a multi-formalism parsing environment for grammar engineering. In *Proc. of the WGEAF08*.

H. Kautz and B. Selman. 1999. Unifying SAT-based and graph-based planning. In *Proc. of IJCAI99*, pages 318–325.

A. Koller, R. Debusmann, M. Gabsdil, and K. Striegnitz. 2004. Put my galakmid coin into the dispenser and kick it: Computational linguistics and theorem proving in a computer game. *JoLLI*, 13(2):187–206.

J. Kreutel and C. Matheson. 2003. Context-dependent interpretation and implicit dialogue acts. In *Perspectives on Dialogue in the New Millenium*, pages 179–192. John Benjamins.

D. Lewis. 1979. Scorekeeping in a language game. *Philosophical Logic*, 8:339–359.

R. Petrick and F. Bacchus. 2004. Extending the knowledge-based approach to planning with incomplete information and sensing. In *Proc. of ICP-KRR04*, pages 613–622.

R. Thomason, M. Stone, and D. DeVault. 2006. Enlightened update: A computational architecture for presupposition and other pragmatic phenomena. In *Proc. of Workshop on Presup. Accommodation*.

CBSEAS, a Summarization System
Integration of Opinion Mining Techniques to Summarize Blogs

Aurélien Bossard, Michel Généreux and **Thierry Poibeau**
Laboratoire d'Informatique de Paris-Nord
CNRS UMR 7030 and Université Paris 13
93430 Villetaneuse — France
{firstname.lastname}@lipn.univ-paris13.fr

Abstract

In this paper, we present a novel approach for automatic summarization. Our system, called CBSEAS, integrates a new method to detect redundancy at its very core, and produce more expressive summaries than previous approaches. Moreover, we show that our system is versatile enough to integrate opinion mining techniques, so that it is capable of producing opinion oriented summaries. The very competitive results obtained during the last Text Evaluation Conference (TAC 2008) show that our approach is efficient.

1 Introduction

During the past decade, automatic summarization, supported by evaluation campaigns and a large research community, has shown fast and deep improvements. Indeed, the research in this domain is guided by strong industrial needs: fast processing despite ever increasing amount of data.

In this paper, we present a novel approach for automatic summarization. Our system, called CBSEAS, integrates a new method to detect redundancy at its very core, and produce more expressive summaries than previous approaches. The system is flexible enough to produce opinion oriented summaries by accommodating techniques to mine documents that express different views or commentaries. The very competitive results obtained during the last Text Evaluation Conference (TAC 2008) show that our approach is efficient.

This short paper is structured as follows: we first give a quick overview of the state of the art. We then describe our system, focusing on the most important novel features implemented. Lastly, we give the details of the results obtained on the TAC 2008 Opinion Pilot task.

2 Related works

Interest in creating automatic summaries has begun in the 1950s (Luhn, 1958). (Edmundson and Wyllys, 1961) proposed features to assign a score to each sentence of a corpus in order to rank these sentences. The ones with the highest scores are kept to produce the summary. The features they used were sentence position (in a news article for example, the first sentences are the most important), proper names and keywords in the document title, indicative phrases and sentence length.

Later on, summarizers aimed at eliminating redundancy, especially for multi-documents summarizing purpose. Identifying redundancy is a critical task, as information appearing several times in different documents can be qualified as important.

Among recent approaches, the "centroid-based summarization" method developed by (Radev et al., 2004) consists in identifying the centroid of a cluster of documents, in other words the terms which best suit the documents to summarize. Then, the sentences to be extracted are the ones that contain the greatest number of centroids. Radev implemented this method in an online multi-document summarizer, MEAD.

Radev further improved MEAD using a different method to extract sentences: "Graph-based centrality" extractor (Erkan and Radev, 2004). It consists in computing similarity between sentences, and then selecting sentences which are considered as "central" in a graph where nodes are sentences and edges are similarities. Sentence selection is then performed by picking the sentences which have been visited most after a random walk on the graph.

The last two systems are dealing with redundancy as a post-processing step. (Zhu et al., 2007), assuming that redundancy should be the concept on what is based multi-document summarization, offered a method to deal with redundancy at the

Proceedings of the EACL 2009 Demonstrations Session, pages 5–8,
Athens, Greece, 3 April 2009.

same time as sentence selection. For that purpose, the authors used a "Markov absorbing chain random walk" on a graph representing the different sentences of the corpus to summarize.

MMR-MD, introduced by Carbonnel in (Carbonell and Goldstein, 1998), is a measure which needs a passage clustering: all passages considered as synonyms are grouped into the same clusters. MMR-MD takes into account the similarity to a query, coverage of a passage (clusters that it belongs to), content in the passage, similarity to passages already selected for the summary, belonging to a cluster or to a document that has already contributed a passage to the summary.

The problem of this measure lies in the clustering method: in the literature, clustering is generally fulfilled using a threshold. If a passage has a similarity to a cluster centroid higher than a threshold, then it is added to this cluster. This makes it a supervised clustering method; an unsupervised clustering method is best suited for automatic summarization, as the corpora we need to summarize are different from one to another. Moreover, sentence synonymy is also dependent on the corpus granularity and on the user compression requirement.

3 CBSEAS: A Clustering-Based Sentence Extractor for Automatic Summarization

We assume that, in multi-document summarization, redundant pieces of information are the single most important element to produce a good summary. Therefore, the sentences which carry those pieces of information have to be extracted. Detecting these sentences conveying the same information is the first step of our approach. The developed algorithm first establishes the similarities between all sentences of the documents to summarize, then applies a clustering algorithm — fast global k-means (López-Escobar et al., 2006) — to the similarity matrix in order to create clusters in which sentences convey the same information.

First, our system ranks all the sentences according to their similarity to the documents centroid. We have chosen to build up the documents centroid with the m most important terms, their importance being reflected by the tf/idf of each term. We then select the n^2 best ranked sentences to create a n sentences long summary. We do so because the clustering algorithm we use to detect sentences

for all $e_j in E$
    $C_1 \leftarrow e_j$
for i from 1 to k do
    for j from 1 to i
        center(C_j) $\leftarrow e_m | e_m maximizes \sum_{e_n in C_j} sim(e_m, e_n)$
    for all e_j in E
        $e_j \rightarrow C_l | C_l maximizes\ sim(center(C_l, e_j))$
    add a new cluster: C_i. It initially contains only its
    center, the worst represented element in its cluster.
done

Figure 1: Fast global k-means algorithm

conveying the same information, fast global k-means, behaves better when it has to group n^2 elements into n clusters. The similarity with the centroid is a weighted sum of terms appearing in both centroid and sentence, normalized by sentence length.

Similarity between sentences is computed using a variant of the "Jaccard" measure. If two terms are not equal, we test their synonymy/hyperonymy using the Wordnet taxonomy (Fellbaum, 1998). In case they are synonyms or hyperonym/hyponym, these terms are taken into account in the similarity calculation, but weighted respectively half and quarter in order to reflect that term equality is more important than term semantic relation. We do this in order to solve the problem pointed out in (Erkan and Radev, 2004) (synonymy was not taken into account for sentence similarity measures) and so to enhance sentence similarity measure. It is crucial to our system based on redundancy location as redundancy assumption is dependent on sentence similarities.

Once the similarities are computed, we cluster the sentences using fast global k-means (description of the algorithm is in figure 1) using the similarity matrix. It works well on a small data set with a small number of dimensions, although it has not yet scaled up as well as we would have expected.

This clustering step completed, we select one sentence per cluster in order to produce a summary that contains most of the relevant information/ideas in the original documents. We do so by choosing the central sentence in each cluster. The central sentence is the one which maximizes the sum of similarities with the other sentences of its cluster. It should be the one that characterizes best the cluster in terms of information vehicled.

4 TAC 2008: The Opinion Summarization Task

In order to evaluate our system, we participated in the Text Analysis Conference (TAC) that proposed in 2008 an opinion summarization task. The goal is to produce fluent and well-organized summaries of blogs. These summaries are oriented by complex user queries, such as "Why do people like.....?" or "Why do people prefer... to...?".

The results were analyzed manually, using the PYRAMID method (Lin et al., 2006): the PYRAMID score of a summary depends on the number of simple semantic units, units considered as important by the annotators. The TAC evaluation for this task also included grammaticality, non-redundancy, structure/coherence and overall fluency scores.

5 CBSEAS Adaptation to the Opinion Summarization Task

Blog summarization is very different from a newswire article or a scientific paper summarization. Linguistic quality as well as reasoning structure are variable from one blogger to another. We cannot use generalities on blog structure, neither on linguistic markers to improve our summarization system. The other problem with blogs is the noise due to the use of unusual language. We had to clean the blogs in a pre-processing step: sentences with a ratio *number of frequent words/total number of words* below a given threshold (0.35) were deemed too noisy and discarded. Frequent words are the one hundred most frequent words in the English language which on average make up approximately half of written texts (Fry et al., 2000).

Our system, CBSEAS, is a "standard" summarization system. We had to adapt it in order to deal with the specific task of summarizing opinions. All sentences from the set of documents to summarize were tagged following the opinion detected in the blog post they originated from. We used for that purpose a two-class (positive or negative) SVM classifier trained on movie reviews. The idea behind the opinion classifier is to improve summaries by selecting sentences having the same opinionated polarity as the query, which were tagged using a SVM trained on the manually tagged queries from the training data provided earlier in TAC.

As the Opinion Summarization Task was to produce a query-oriented summary, the sentence preselection was changed, using the user query instead of the documents centroid. We also changed the sentence pre-selection ranking measure by weighting terms according to their lexical category; we have chosen to give more weight to proper names than verbs adjectives, adverbs and nouns. Indeed, opinions we had to summarize were mostly on products or people.

While experimenting our system on TAC 2008 training data, we noticed that extracting sentences which are closest to their cluster center was not satisfactory. Some other sentences in the same cluster were best fitted to a query-oriented summary. We added the sentence ranking used for the sentence pre-selection to the final sentence extractor. Each sentence is given a score which is the distance to the cluster center times the similarity to the query.

6 TAC 2008 Results on Opinion Summarization Task

Participants to the Opinion Summarization Task were allowed to use extra-information given by TAC organizers. These pieces of information are called snippets. The snippets contain the relevant information, and could be used as a stand-alone dataset. Participants were classified into two different groups: one for those who did not use snippets, and one for those who did. We did not use snippets at all, as it is a more realistic challenge to look directly at the blogs with no external help. The results we present here are those of the participants that were not using snippets. Indeed, systems using snippets obtained much higher scores than the other systems. We cannot compare our system to systems using snippets.

Our system obtained quite good results on the "opinion task": the scores can be found on figure 2. As one can see, our responsiveness scores are low compared to the others (responsiveness score corresponds to the following question: "*How much would you pay for that summary?*"). We suppose that despite the grammaticality, fluency and pyramid scores of our summaries, judges gave a bad responsiveness score to our summaries because they are too long: we made the choice to produce summaries with a compression rate of 10% when it was possible, the maximum length authorized otherwise.

Evaluation	CBSEAS	Mean	Best	Worst	Rank
Pyramid	.169	.151	.251	.101	5/20
Grammatic.	5.95	5.14	7.54	3.54	3/20
Non-redun.	6.64	5.88	7.91	4.36	4/20
Structure	3.50	2.68	3.59	2.04	2/20
Fluency	4.45	3.43	5.32	2.64	2/20
Responsiv.	2.64	2.61	5.77	1.68	8/20

Figure 2: Opinion task overall results

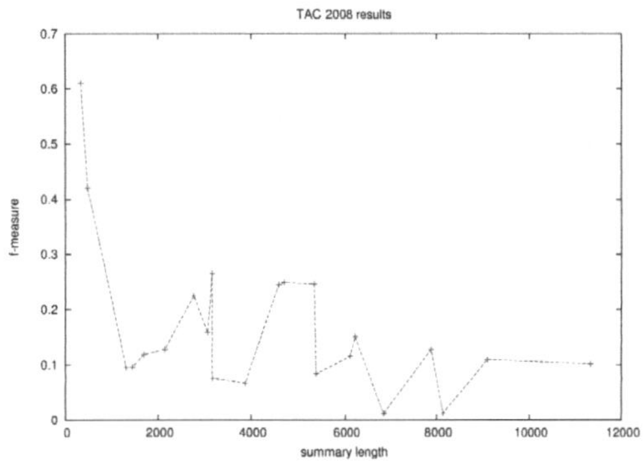

Figure 3: Opinion task results

However, we noticed that the quality of our summaries was very erratic. We assume this is due to the length of our summaries, as the longest summaries are the ones which get the worst scores in terms of pyramid f-score (fig 3). The length of the summaries is a ratio of the original documents length. The quality of the summaries would be decreasing while the number of input sentences is increasing.

Solutions to fix this problem could be:

- Define a better score for the correspondence to a user query and remove sentences which are under a threshold;
- Extract sentences from the clusters that contain more than a predefined number of elements only.

This would result in improving the pertinence of the extracted sentences. The users reading the summaries would also be less disturbed by the large amount of sentences a too long summary provides. As the "opinion summarization" task was evaluated manually and reflects well the quality of a summary for an operational use, the conclusions of this evaluation are good indicators of the quality of the summaries produced by our system.

7 Conclusion

We presented here a new approach for multi-document summarization. It uses an unsupervised clustering method to group semantically related sentences together. It can be compared to approaches using sentence neighbourhood (Erkan and Radev, 2004), because the sentences which are highly related to the highest number of sentences are those which will be extracted first. However, our approach is different since sentence selection is directly dependent on redundancy location. Also, redundancy elimination, which is crucial in multi-document summarization, takes place in the same step as sentence selection.

References

Jaime Carbonell and Jade Goldstein. 1998. The use of MMR, diversity-based reranking for reordering documents and producing summaries. In *SIGIR'98*, pages 335–336, New York, NY, USA. ACM.

Harold P. Edmundson and Ronald E. Wyllys. 1961. Automatic abstracting and indexing—survey and recommendations. *Commun. ACM*, 4(5):226–234.

Güneş Erkan and Dragomir R. Radev. 2004. Lexrank: Graph-based centrality as salience in text summarization. *Journal of Artificial Intelligence Research (JAIR)*.

Christiane Fellbaum. 1998. *WordNet: An Electronic Lexical Database*. MIT Press.

Edward Bernard Fry, Jacqueline E. Kress, and Dona Lee Fountoukidis. 2000. *The Reading Teachers Book of Lists*. Jossey-Bass, 4th edition.

Chin-Yew Lin, Guihong Cao, Jianfeng Gao, and Jian-Yun Nie. 2006. An information-theoretic approach to automatic evaluation of summaries. In *Proceedings of HLT-NAACL*, pages 463–470, Morristown, NJ, USA.

Saúl López-Escobar, Jesús Ariel Carrasco-Ochoa, and José Francisco Martínez Trinidad. 2006. Fast global -means with similarity functions algorithm. In *IDEAL*, volume 4224 of *Springer, Lecture Notes in Computer Science*, pages 512–521.

H.P. Luhn. 1958. The automatic creation of literature abstracts. *IBM Journal*, 2(2):159–165.

Dragomir Radev et al. 2004. MEAD - a platform for multidocument multilingual text summarization. In *Proceedings of LREC 2004*, Lisbon, Portugal.

Xiaojin Zhu, Andrew Goldberg, Jurgen Van Gael, and David Andrzejewski. 2007. Improving diversity in ranking using absorbing random walks. In *Proceedings of HLT-NAACL*, pages 97–104, Rochester, USA.

Grammatical Framework Web Service

Björn Bringert* and **Krasimir Angelov** and **Aarne Ranta**
Department of Computer Science and Engineering
Chalmers University of Technology and University of Gothenburg
{bringert,krasimir,aarne}@chalmers.se

Abstract

We present a web service for natural language parsing, prediction, generation, and translation using grammars in Portable Grammar Format (PGF), the target format of the Grammatical Framework (GF) grammar compiler. The web service implementation is open source, works with any PGF grammar, and with any web server that supports FastCGI. The service exposes a simple interface which makes it possible to use it for interactive natural language web applications. We describe the functionality and interface of the web service, and demonstrate several applications built on top of it.

1 Introduction

Current web applications often consist of JavaScript code that runs in the user's web browser, with server-side code that does the heavy lifting. We present a web service for natural language processing with Portable Grammar Format (PGF, Angelov et al., 2008) grammars, which can be used to build interactive natural language web applications. PGF is the back-end format to which Grammatical Framework (GF, Ranta, 2004) grammars are compiled. PGF has been designed to allow efficient implementations.

The web service has a simple API based solely on HTTP GET requests. It returns responses in JavaScript Object Notation (JSON, Crockford, 2006). The server-side program is distributed as part of the GF software distribution, under the GNU General Public License (GPL). The program is generic, in the sense that it can be used with any PGF grammar without any modification of the program.

2 Grammatical Framework

Grammatical Framework (GF, Ranta, 2004) is a type-theoretical grammar formalism. A GF grammar consists of an *abstract syntax*, which defines a set of abstract syntax trees, and one or more *concrete syntaxes*, which define how abstract syntax trees are mapped to (and from) strings. The process of producing a string (or, more generally, a feature structure) from an abstract syntax tree is called *linearization*. The opposite, producing an abstract syntax tree (or several, if the grammar is ambiguous) from a string is called *parsing*.

In a small, semantically oriented application grammar, the sentence *"2 is even"* may correspond to the abstract syntax tree Even 2. In a larger, more syntactically oriented grammar, in this case the English GF resource grammar (Ranta, 2007), the same sentence can correspond to the abstract syntax tree PhrUtt NoPConj (UttS (UseCl (TTAnt TPres ASimul) PPos (PredVP (UsePN (NumPN (NumDigits (IDig D_2)))) (UseComp (CompAP (PositA *even_A*)))))) NoVoc.

2.1 Portable Grammar Format (PGF)

Portable Grammar Format (PGF, Angelov et al., 2008) is a low-level format to which GF grammars are compiled. The PGF Web Service loads PGF files from disk, and uses them to serve client requests. These PGF files are normally produced by compiling GF grammars, but they could also be produced by other means, for example by a compiler from another grammar formalism. Such compilers currently exist for context-free grammars in BNF and EBNF formats, though they compile via GF.

2.2 Parsing and Word Prediction

For each concrete syntax in a PGF file, there is a parsing grammar, which is a Parallel Multiple Context Free Grammar (PMCFG, Seki et al., 1991). The PGF interpreter uses an efficient parsing algorithm for PMCFG (Angelov, 2009) which is similar to the Earley algorithm for CFG. The algorithm is top-down and incremental which makes it possible to use it for word completion. When the whole sentence is known, the parser just takes the tokens one by one and computes the chart of all possible parse trees. If the sentence is not yet complete, then the known tokens can be used to compute a partial parse chart. Since the algorithm is top-down it is possible to predict the set of valid next tokens by using just the partial chart.

The prediction can be used in applications to guide the user to stay within the coverage of the grammar. At each point the set of valid next tokens is shown and the user can select one of them.

*Now at Google Inc.

Proceedings of the EACL 2009 Demonstrations Session, pages 9–12,
Athens, Greece, 3 April 2009.

Figure 1: Translator interface. This example uses the Bronzeage grammar, which consists of simple syntactic rules along with lexica based on Swadesh lists. Demo at `http://digitalgrammars.com/translate`.

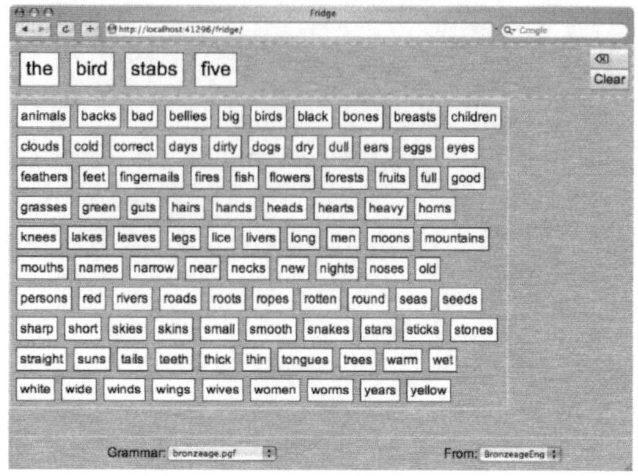

Figure 2: Fridge poetry screenshot. Demo at `http://digitalgrammars.com/fridge`.

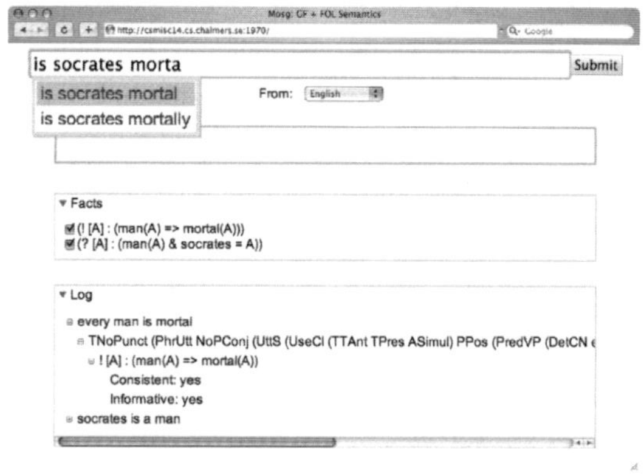

Figure 3: Reasoning screenshot. Demo at `http://digitalgrammars.com/mosg`.

The word prediction is based entirely on the grammar and not on any additional n-gram model. This means that it works with any PGF grammar and no extra work is needed. In addition it works well even with long distance dependencies. For example if the subject is in a particular gender and the verb requires gender agreement, then the the correct form is predicted, independently on how far the verb is from the subject.

3 Applications

Several interactive web applications have been built with the PGF Web Service. They are all JavaScript programs which run in the user's web browser and send asynchronous HTTP requests to the PGF Web Service.

3.1 Translator

The simplest application (see Figure 1) presents the user with a text field for input, and drop-down boxes for selecting the grammar and language to use. For every change in the text field, the application asks the PGF Web Service for a number of possible completions of the input, and displays them below the text field. The user can continue typing, or select one of the suggestions. When the current input can be parsed completely, the input is translated to all available languages.

3.2 Fridge Poetry

The second application is similar in functionality to the first, but it presents a different user interface. The interface (see Figure 2) mimics the popular refrigerator magnet poetry sets. However, in contrast to physical fridge magnets, this application handles inflection automatically and only allows the construction of grammatically correct sentences (as defined by the selected grammar). It also shows translations for complete inputs and allows the user to switch languages.

3.3 Reasoning

Another application is a natural language reasoning system which accepts facts and questions from the users, and tries to answer the questions based on the facts given. The application uses the PGF Web Service to parse inputs. It uses two other web services for semantic interpretation and reasoning, respectively. The semantic interpretation service uses a continuation-based compositional mapping of abstract syntax terms to first-order logic formulas (Bringert, 2008). The reasoning service is a thin layer on top of the Equinox theorem prover and the Paradox model finder (Claessen and Sörensson, 2003).

4 API

Below, we will show URI paths for each function, for example `/pgf/food.pgf/parse`. Arguments to each function are given in the URL query string, in `application/x-www-form-urlencoded` (Raggett et al., 1999) format. Thus, if the service is running on `example.com`, the URI for a request to parse the string "this fish is fresh" using the `FoodEng` concrete syntax in the `food.pgf` grammar would be: `http://example.com/pgf/food.pgf/parse?input=this+fish+is+fresh&from=FoodEng`. The functions described below each accept some subset of the following arguments:

`from` The name of the concrete syntax to parse with or translate from. Multiple `from` arguments can be given, in which case all the specified languages are tried. If omitted, all languages (that can be used for parsing) are used.

`cat` The name of the abstract syntax category to parse or translate in, or generate output in. If omitted, the start category specified in the PGF file is used.

`to` The name of the concrete syntax to linearize or translate to. Multiple `to` arguments can be given, in which case all the specified languages are used. If omitted, results for all languages are returned.

`input` The text to parse, complete or translate. If omitted, the empty string is used.

`tree` The abstract syntax tree to linearize.

`limit` The maximum number of results to return.

All results are returned in UTF-8 encoded JSON or JSONP format. A `jsonp` argument can be given to each function to invoke a callback function when the response is evaluated in a JavaScript interpreter. This makes it possible to circumvent the Same Origin Policy in the web browser and call the PGF Web Service from applications loaded from another server.

4.1 Grammar List

`/pgf` retrieves a list of the available PGF files.

4.2 Grammar Info

`/pgf/grammar.pgf`, where `grammar.pgf` is the name of a PGF file on the server, retrieves information about the given grammar. This information includes the name of the abstract syntax, the categories in the abstract syntax, and the list of concrete syntaxes.

4.3 Parsing

`/pgf/grammar.pgf/parse` parses an input string and returns a number of abstract syntax trees. Optional arguments: `input`, `from`, `cat`.

4.4 Completion

`/pgf/grammar.pgf/complete` returns a list of predictions for the next token, given a partial input. Optional arguments: `input`, `from`, `cat`, `limit`. If `limit` is omitted, all results are returned.

4.5 Linearization

`/pgf/grammar.pgf/linearize` accepts an abstract syntax tree, and returns the results of linearizing it to one or more languages. Mandatory arguments: `tree`. Optional arguments: `to`.

4.6 Random Generation

`/pgf/grammar.pgf/random` generates a number of randomly generated abstract syntax trees for the selected grammar. Optional arguments: `cat`, `limit`. If `limit` is omitted, one tree is returned.

4.7 Translation

`/pgf/grammar.pgf/translate` performs text to text translation. This is done by parsing, followed by linearization. Optional arguments: `input`, `from`, `cat`, `to`.

5 Application to Controlled Languages

The use of controlled languages is becoming more popular with the development of Web and Semantic Web technologies. Related projects include Attempto (Attempto, 2008), CLOnE (Funk et al., 2007), and Common Logic Controlled English (CLCE) (Sowa, 2004). All these projects provide languages which are subsets of English and have semantic translations into first order logic (CLCE), OWL (CLOnE) or both (Attempto). In the case of Attempto, the translation is into first order logic and if it is possible to the weaker OWL language.

The general idea is that since the controlled language is a subset of some other language it should be understandable to everyone without special training. The opposite is not true - not every English sentence is a valid sentence in the controlled language and the user must learn how to stay within its limitations. Although this is a disadvantage, in practice it is much easier to remember some subset of English phrases rather than to learn a whole new formal language. Word suggestion functionality such as that in the PGF Web Service can help the user stay within the controlled fragment.

In contrast to the above mentioned systems, GF is not a system which provides only one controlled language, but a framework within which the developer can develop his own language. The task is simplified by the existence of a resource grammar library (Ranta, 2007) which takes care of all low-level details such as word order, and gender, number or case agreement. In fact, the language developer does not have to be skilled in linguistics, but does have to be a domain expert and can concentrate on the specific task.

Most controlled language frameworks are focused on some subset of English while other languages receive very little or no attention. With GF, the controlled language does not have to be committed to only one natural language but could have a parallel grammar with realizations into many languages. In this case the user could choose whether to use the English version or, for example, the French version, and still produce the same abstract representation.

6 Implementation

The PGF Web Service is a FastCGI program written in Haskell. The program is a thin layer on top of the PGF interpreter, which implements all the PGF functionality, such as parsing, completion and linearization. The web service also uses external libraries for FastCGI communication, and JSON and UTF-8 encoding and decoding.

The main advantage of using FastCGI instead of plain CGI is that the PGF file does not have to be reloaded for each request. Instead, each PGF file is loaded the first time it is requested, and after that, it is only reloaded if the file on disk is changed.

7 Performance

The web service layer introduces minimal overhead. The typical response time for a parse request with a small grammar, when running on a typical current PC, is around 1 millisecond. For large grammars, response times can be on the order of several seconds, but this is entirely dependent on the PGF interpreter implementation.

The server is multi-threaded, with one lightweight thread for each client request. A single instance of the server can run threads on all cores of a multi-core processor. Since the server maintains no state and requires no synchronization, it can be easily replicated on multiple machines with load balancing. Since all requests are cacheable HTTP GET requests, a caching proxy could be used to improve performance if it is expected that there will be repeated requests for the same URI.

8 Future Work

The abstract syntax in GF is based on Martin Löf's (1984) type theory and supports dependent types. They can be used go beyond the pure syntax and to check the sentences for semantic consistency. The current parser completely ignores dependent types. This means that the word prediction will suggest completions which might not be semantically meaningful.

In order to improve performance for high-traffic applications that use large grammars, the web service could cache responses. As long as the grammar is not modified, identical requests will always produce identical responses.

9 Conclusions

We have presented a web service for grammar-based natural language processing, which can be used to build interactive natural language web applications. The web service has a simple API, based on HTTP GET requests with JSON responses. The service allows high levels of performance and scalability, and has been used to build several applications.

References

Krasimir Angelov. 2009. Incremental Parsing with Parallel Multiple Context-Free Grammars. In *European Chapter of the Association for Computational Linguistics*.

Krasimir Angelov, Björn Bringert, and Aarne Ranta. 2008. PGF: A Portable Run-Time Format for Type-Theoretical Grammars. *Journal of Logic, Language and Information*, submitted. URL `http://www.cs.chalmers.se/~bringert/publ/pgf/pgf.pdf`.

Attempto. 2008. Attempto Project Homepage - http://attempto.ifi.uzh.ch/site/. URL `http://attempto.ifi.uzh.ch/site/`.

Björn Bringert. 2008. Delimited Continuations, Applicative Functors and Natural Language Semantics. URL `http://www.cs.chalmers.se/~bringert/publ/continuation-semantics/continuation-semantics.pdf`.

Koen Claessen and Niklas Sörensson. 2003. New Techniques that Improve MACE-style Model Finding. In *Workshop on Model Computation (MODEL)*. URL `http://www.cs.chalmers.se/~koen/pubs/model-paradox.ps`.

Douglas Crockford. 2006. The application/json Media Type for JavaScript Object Notation (JSON). RFC 4627 (Informational). URL `http://www.ietf.org/rfc/rfc4627.txt`.

Adam Funk, Valentin Tablan, Kalina Bontcheva, Hamish Cunningham, Brian Davis, and Siegfried Handschuh. 2007. CLOnE: Controlled Language for Ontology Editing. In *Proceedings of the International Semantic Web Conference (ISWC 2007)*. Busan, Korea.

Per Martin-Löf. 1984. *Intuitionistic Type Theory*. Bibliopolis, Naples.

Dave Raggett, Arnaud Le Hors, and Ian Jacobs. 1999. HTML 4.01 Specification. Technical report, W3C. URL `http://www.w3.org/TR/1999/REC-html401-19991224/`.

Aarne Ranta. 2004. Grammatical Framework: A Type-Theoretical Grammar Formalism. *Journal of Functional Programming*, 14(2):145–189. URL `http://dx.doi.org/10.1017/S0956796803004738`.

Aarne Ranta. 2007. Modular Grammar Engineering in GF. *Research on Language and Computation*, 5(2):133–158. URL `http://dx.doi.org/10.1007/s11168-007-9030-6`.

Hiroyuki Seki, Takashi Matsumura, Mamoru Fujii, and Tadao Kasami. 1991. On multiple context-free grammars. *Theoretical Computer Science*, 88(2):191–229. URL `http://dx.doi.org/10.1016/0304-3975(91)90374-B`.

John Sowa. 2004. Common Logic Controlled English. Draft. URL `http://www.jfsowa.com/clce/specs.htm`.

GOSSIP GALORE

A Self-Learning Agent for Exchanging Pop Trivia

Xiwen Cheng, Peter Adolphs, Feiyu Xu, Hans Uszkoreit, Hong Li
DFKI GmbH, Language Technology Lab
Stuhlsatzenhausweg 3, D-66123 Saarbrücken, Germany
{xiwen.cheng,peter.adolphs,feiyu,uszkoreit,lihong}@domain.com

Abstract

This paper describes a self-learning software agent who collects and learns knowledge from the web and also exchanges her knowledge via dialogues with the users. The agent is built on top of information extraction, web mining, question answering and dialogue system technologies, and users can freely formulate their questions within the gossip domain and obtain the answers in multiple ways: textual response, graph-based visualization of the related concepts and speech output.

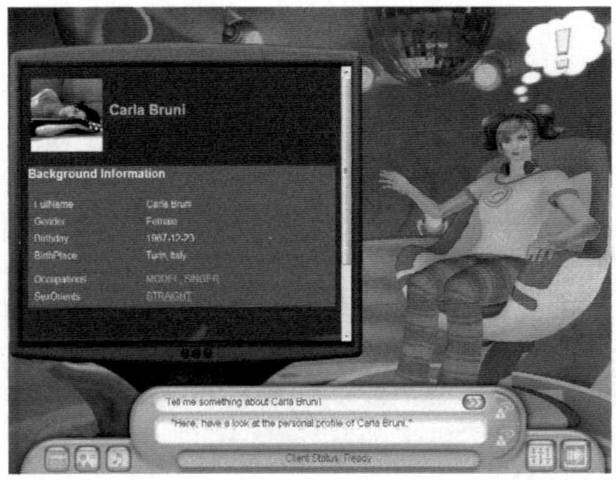

Figure 1: Gossip Galore responding to "Tell me something about Carla Bruni!"

1 Introduction

The system presented here is developed within the project *Responsive Artificial Situated Cognitive Agents Living and Learning on the Internet* (RASCALLI) supported by the European Commission Cognitive Systems Programme (IST-27596-2004). The goal of the project is to develop and implement cognitively enhanced artificial agents, using technologies in natural language processing, question answering, web-based information extraction, semantic web and interaction driven profiling with cognitive modelling (Krenn, 2008).

This paper describes a conversational agent "Gossip Galore", an active self-learning system that can learn, update and interpret information from the web, and can make conversations with users and provide answers to their questions in the domain of celebrity gossip. In more detail, by applying a minimally supervised relation extraction system (Xu et al., 2007; Xu et al., 2008), the agent automatically collects the knowledge from relevant websites, and also communicates with the users using a question-answering engine via a 3D graphic interface.

This paper is organized as follows. Section 2 gives an overview of the system architecture and presents the design and functionalities of the components. Section 3 explains the system setup and discusses implementation details, and finally Section 4 draws conclusions.

2 System Overview

Figure 1 shows a use case of the system. Given a query "Tell me something about Carla Bruni", the application would trigger a series of background actions and respond with: "Here, have a look at the personal profile of Carla Bruni". Meanwhile, the personal profile of Carla Bruni, would be displayed on the screen. The design of the interface reflects the domain of celebrity gossip: the agent is depicted as a young lady in 3D graphics, who communicates with users. As an additional feature, users can access the dialogue memory of the system, which simulates the human memory in dialogues. An example of the dialogue memory is sketched in Figure 2.

As shown in Figure 3, the system consists of a number of components. In principle, first, a user's query is linguistically analyzed, and then inter-

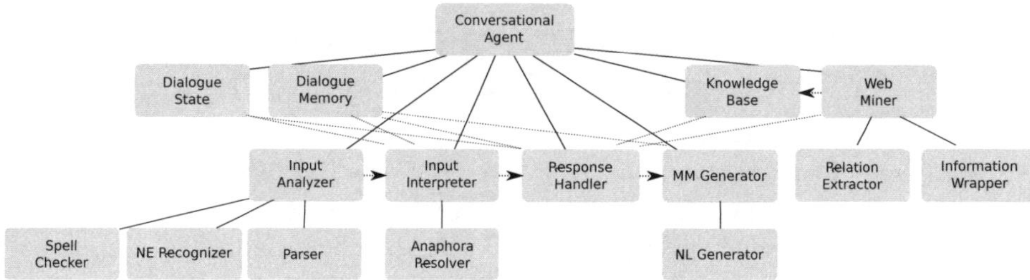

Figure 3: Agent architecture and interaction of components

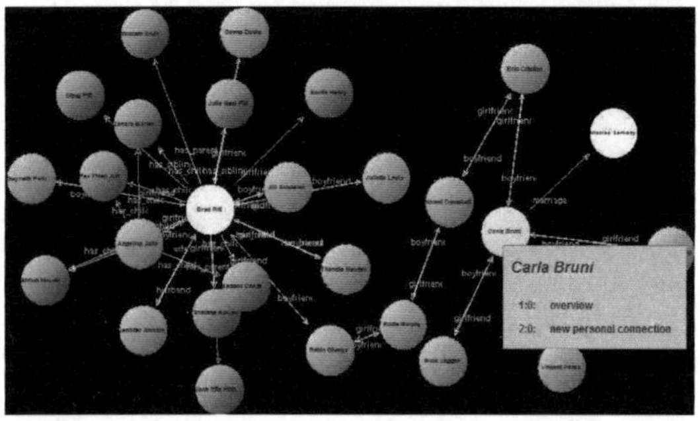

Figure 2: Representation of Social Network in Dialogue Memory

preted with respect to the context of the dialogue. A Response Handler will then consult the knowledge base pre-constructed by extracting relevant information from the Web, and pass the answer, in an abstract representation, to a Multimodal Generator, which realizes and presents the answer to the user in multiple ways. The main components are described in the following sections.

2.1 Knowledge Base

The knowledge base is automatically built by the Web Miner. It contains knowledge regarding properties of persons or groups and their social relationships. The persons and groups that we concern are celebrities in the entertainment industry (e.g., singers, bands, or movie stars) and their relatives (e.g., partners) and friends. Typical properties of a person include name, gender, birthday, etc., and profiles of celebrities contain additional properties such as sexual orientation, home pages, stage names, genres of their work, albums, and prizes. Social relationships between the persons/groups such as parent-child, partner, sibling, influencing/influenced and group-member, are also stored.

2.2 Web Miner

The Web Miner fetches relevant concepts and their relations by means of two technologies: a) information wrapping for exaction of personal profiles from structured and semi-structured web content, and b) a minimally supervised machine learning method provided by DARE (Xu et al., 2007; Xu et al., 2008) to acquire relations from free texts. DARE learns linguistic patterns indicating the target semantic relations by taking some relation instances as initial seed. For example, assume that the following seed for a parent-child relationship is given to the DARE system:

(1) **Seed**: ⟨Angelina Jolie, Shiloh Nouvel Jolie-Pitt, daughter⟩

One sentence that matches the entities mentioned in the seed above could be (2), and from which the DARE system can derive a linguistic pattern as shown in 3.

(2) **Matched sentence**: *Angelina Jolie* and Brad Pitt welcome their new *daughter Shiloh Nouvel Jolie-Pitt.*

(3) **Extracted pattern**: ⟨subject: celebrity⟩ welcome ⟨mod: "new daughter"⟩ ⟨object: person⟩

Given the learned pattern, new instances of the "parent-child" relationship can be automatically discovered, e.g.:

(4) **New acquired instances**: ⟨Adam Sandler, Sunny Madeline⟩ ⟨Cynthia Rodriguez, Ella Alexander⟩

Given the discovered relations among the celebrities and other people, the system constructs a social network, which is the basis for providing answers to users' questions regarding celebrities' relationships. The network also serves as a resource for the active dialogue memory of the agent as shown in Figure 2.

2.3 Input Analyzer and Input Interpreter

The Input Analyzer is designed as both domain and dialogue context independent. It relies on several linguistic analysis tools: 1) a spell checker, 2) a named entity recognizer SProUT (Drozdzynski et al., 2004), and 3) a syntactic parsing component for which we currently employ a fuzzy paraphrase matcher to approximate the output of a deep syntactic/semantic parser.

In contrast to the Input Analyzer, the Input Interpreter analyzes the input with respect to the context of the dialogue. It contains two major components: 1) anaphoric resolution, which refers pronouns to previously mentioned entities with the help of the dialogue memory, and 2) domain classification, which determines whether the entities contained in a user query can be found in the gossip knowledge base (cf. "Carla Bruni" vs. "Nicolas Sarkozy") and whether the answer focus belongs to the domain (cf. "stage name" vs "body guard"). For example, a simple factoid query such as "Who is Madonna", an embedded questions like "I wonder who Madonna is", and expressions of requests and wishes such as "I'm interested in Madonna", would share the same answer focus, i.e., the "personal profile" of "Madonna". In addition to the simple answer types such as "person name", "location" and "date/time", our system can also deal with complex answer focus types such as "personal profile", "social network" and "relation path", as well as domain-relevant concepts such as "party affiliation" or "sexual orientation".

Finally, the analysis of each query is associated with a meaning representation, an answer focus and an expected answer type.

2.4 Response Handler

This component executes the planned action based on the properties of the answer focus and the entities in a query. In cases where the answer focus or the entities cannot be found in the knowledge base, the system would still attempt to provide a constructive answer. For instance, if a question contains a domain-specific answer focus but entities unknown to the knowledge base, the agent will automatically look for alternative knowledge resources, e.g., Wikipedia. For example, given the question "Tell me something about Nicolas Sarkozy!", the agent would attempt a Web search and return the corresponding page on Wikipedia about "Nicolas Sarkozy", even if the knowledge base does not contain his information since he is a politician rather than an entertainer.

In addition, specific strategies have been developed to deal with negative answers. For instance, the agent would answer the question: *When did Madonna die?*, with "As far as I know, Madonna is still alive.", as it cannot find any information regarding Madonna's death.

2.5 Multimodal Generator

The agent (i.e., the young lady in Figure 1) is equipped with multimodal capabilities to interact with users. It can show the results in textual and speech forms, using body gestures, facial expressions, and finally via multimedia output to an embedded screen. We currently employ template-based generators for producing both the natural language utterances and the instructions to the agent that controls the multimodal communication with the user.

2.6 Dialogue State

The responsibility of this component is to keep track of the current state of the dialogue between a user and the agent. It models the system's expectation of the user's next action and the system's reactions. For example, if a user misspelled a name as in the question "Who is Roby Williams?", the system would answer with a clarification question: "Did you mean Robbie Williams?" The user is then expected to react to the question with either "yes" or "no", which would not be interpretable in other dialogue contexts where the user is expected to ask a question. The fact that the system asks a clarification question and expects a yes/no answer as well as the repaired question are stored in the Dialogue State component.

2.7 Dialogue Memory

This component aims to simulate the cognitive capacity of the memory of a human being: construction of a short-time memory and activation of long-time memory (our Knowledge Base). It records the sequence of all entities mentioned during the conversation and their respective target foci. Simultaneously, it retrieves all the related information from the Knowledge Base. In figure 2, the dialogue memory for the three questions "Tell me something about Carla Bruni.", "Can you tell me some news about her?", "How many kids does Brad Pitt have?" is shown. Green and yellow bubbles are entities mentioned in the dialogue context, where the yellow one is the last mentioned entity. White bubbles indicate the newest records which are acquired in the last process of online QA.

3 Implementation

The system uses a client-server architecture. The server is responsible for accepting new connections, managing accounts, processing conversations and passing responses to the clients. All the server-side functions are implemented in Java 1.6. We use Jetty as a web server to deliver multimedia representations of an answer and to provide selected functionalities of the system as web services to our partners. The knowledge base is stored in a MySQL database whose size is 11MB, and contains information of 38,758 persons including 16,532 artists and 1,407 music groups. As for the social connection data, there are 14,909 parent-child, 16,886 partner, 4,214 sibling, 308 influence/influenced and 9,657 group-member relational pairs. The social network is visualized in JGraph, and speech output is generated by the open-source speech synthesis system *OpenMary* (Schröder and Hunecke, 2007).

There are two interfaces realizing the client-side of the system: a 3D software application and a web interface. The software application uses a 3D computer game engine, and communicates with the server by messages in an XML format based on BML and SSML. In addition, we provide a web interface[1], implemented using HTML and Javascript on the browser side, and Java Servlets on the server side, offering the same core functionality as the 3D client.

Both the server and the web client are platform independent. The 3D client runs on Windows with a dedicated 3D graphics card. The recommended memory for the server is 1GB.

4 Conclusions

This paper describes a fully implemented software application, which discovers and learns information and knowledge from the Web, and communicates with users and exchanges gossip trivia with them. The system uses many novel technologies in order to achieve the goal of vividly chatting and interacting with the users in a fun way. The technologies include information extraction, question answering, dialogue modeling, response planning and multimodal presentation generation. Please refer to (Xu et al., 2009) for additional details about the "Gossip Galore" system.

The planned future extensions include the integration of deeper language processing methods to discover more precise linguistic patterns. A prime candidate for this extension is our own deep syntactic/semantic parser. Another plan concerns the required temporal aspects of relations together with credibility checking. Finally, we plan to exploit the dialogue memory for moving more of the dialogue initiative to the agent. In cases of missing or negative answers or in cases of pauses on the user side, the agent can use the active parts of the dialogue memory to propose additional relevant information or to guide the user to fruitful requests within the range of user's interests.

References

Witold Drozdzynski, Hans-Ulrich Krieger, Jakub Piskorski, Ulrich Schäfer, and Feiyu Xu. 2004. Shallow processing with unification and typed feature structures – foundations and applications. *Künstliche Intelligenz*, 1:17–23.

Brigitte Krenn. 2008. Responsive artificial situated cognitive agents living and learning on the internet, April. Poster presented at CogSys 2008.

Marc Schröder and Anna Hunecke. 2007. Mary tts participation in the Blizzard Challenge 2007. In *Proceedings of the Blizzard Challenge 2007*, Bonn, Germany.

Feiyu Xu, Hans Uszkoreit, and Hong Li. 2007. A seed-driven bottom-up machine learning framework for extracting relations of various complexity. *Proceedings of ACL-2007*, pages 584–591.

Feiyu Xu, Hans Uszkoreit, and Hong Li. 2008. Task driven coreference resolution for relation extraction. In *Proceedings of ECAI 2008*, Patras, Greece.

Feiyu Xu, Peter Adolphs, Hans Uszkoreit, Xiwen Cheng, and Hong Li. 2009. Gossip galore: A conversational web agent for collecting and sharing pop trivia. In *Joaquim Filipe, Ana Fred, and Bernadette Sharp (eds). Proceedings of ICAART 2009*, Porto, Portugal.

[1] `http://rascalli.dfki.de/live/dialogue.page`

An Open-Source Natural Language Generator for OWL Ontologies and its Use in Protégé and Second Life

Dimitrios Galanis*, **George Karakatsiotis***, **Gerasimos Lampouras***, **Ion Androutsopoulos***+
*Department of Informatics, Athens University of Economics and Business, Athens, Greece
+Digital Curation Unit, Research Centre "Athena", Athens, Greece

Abstract

We demonstrate an open-source natural language generation engine that produces descriptions of entities and classes in English and Greek from OWL ontologies that have been annotated with linguistic and user modeling information expressed in RDF. We also demonstrate an accompanying plug-in for the Protégé ontology editor, which can be used to create the ontology's annotations and generate previews of the resulting texts by invoking the generation engine. The engine has been embedded in robots acting as museum tour guides in the physical world and in Second Life; here we demonstrate the latter application.

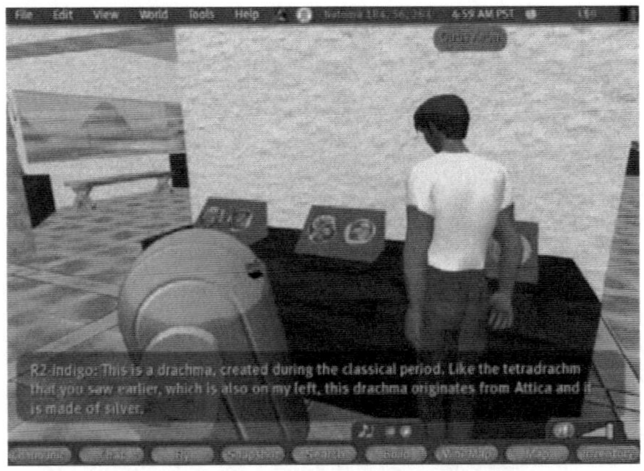

Figure 1: Generating texts in Second Life.

1 Introduction

NaturalOWL (Galanis and Androutsopoulos, 2007; Androutsopoulos and Galanis, 2008) is a natural language generation engine that produces descriptions of entitities (e.g., items for sale, museum exhibits) and classes (e.g., types of exhibits) in English and Greek from OWL DL ontologies; the ontologies must have been annotated with linguistic and user modeling annotations expressed in RDF.[1] An accompanying plug-in for the well known Protégé ontology editor is available, which can be used to create the linguistic and user modeling annotations while editing an ontology, as well as to generate previews of the resulting texts by invoking the generation engine.[2]

NaturalOWL is based on ideas from ILEX (O'Donnell et al., 2001) and M-PIRO (Isard et al., 2003; Androutsopoulos et al., 2007), but it uses templates instead of systemic grammars, it is publicly available as open-source software, it is written entirely in Java, and it provides native support for OWL ontologies, making it particularly useful for Semantic Web applications (Antoniou and van Harmelen, 2004).[3] Well known advantages of natural language generation (Reiter and Dale, 2000) include the ability to generate texts in multiple languages from the same ontology; and the ability to tailor the semantic content and language expressions of the texts to the user type (e.g., child vs. adult) and the interaction history (e.g., by avoiding repetitions, or by comparing to previous objects).

In project XENIOS (Vogiatzis et al., 2008), NaturalOWL was embedded in a mobile robot acting as a museum guide, and in project INDIGO it is being integrated in a more advanced robotic guide that includes a multimodal dialogue manager, facial animation, and mechanisms to recognize and express emotions (Konstantopoulos et al., 2009). Here, we demonstrate a similar application, where NaturalOWL is embedded in a robotic avatar acting

[1]See `http://www.w3.org/TR/owl-features/` for information on OWL and its versions. For information on RDF, consult `http://www.w3.org/RDF/`.

[2]M-PIRO's authoring tool (Androutsopoulos et al., 2007), now called ELEON (Bilidas et al., 2007), can also be used; see `http://www.iit.demokritos.gr/skel/`.

[3]NaturalOWL comes with a GNU General Public License (GPL). The software can be downloaded from `http://nlp.cs.aueb.gr/`.

Proceedings of the EACL 2009 Demonstrations Session, pages 17–20,
Athens, Greece, 3 April 2009.

as a museum guide in Second Life (Oberlander et al., 2008), as shown in figure 1. We also demonstrate how the underlying ontology of the museum and its linguistic and user modeling annotations can be edited in Protégé.

2 NaturalOWL's architecture

NaturalOWL adopts a typical natural language generation pipeline (Reiter and Dale, 2000). It produces texts in three stages: document planning, microplanning, and surface realization.

In document planning, the system first selects from the ontology the logical facts (OWL triples) that will be conveyed to the user, taking into account interest scores manually assigned to the facts via the annotations of the ontology, as well as a dynamcally updated user model that shows what information has already been conveyed to the user. Logical facts that report similarities or differences to previously encountered entities may also be included in the output of content selection, giving rise to comparisons like the one in figure 1. The selected facts are then ordered using a manually specified partial order, which is also part of the ontology's annotations.

In micro-planning, the system turns each selected fact into a sentence by using micro-plans, in effect patterns that leave referring expressions underspecified. Figure 2 shows a micro-plan being edited with NaturalOWL's Protégé plug-in. The micro-plan specifies that to express a fact that involves the `made-of` property, the system should concatenate an automatically generated referring expression (e.g., name, pronoun, definite noun phrase) in nominative case for the owner of the fact (semantic subject of the triple), the verb form "is made" (or "are made", if the subject is in plural), the preposition "of", and then another automatically generated referring expression in accusative case for the filler of the property (semantic object). The referring expressions are generated by taking into account the context of each sentence, attempting to avoid repetitions without introducing ambiguities. Domain-independent aggregation rules are then employed to combine the resulting sentences into longer ones.

In surface realization, the final form of the text is produced; it can be marked up automatically with tags that indicate punctuation symbols, grammatical categories, the logical facts expressed by the sentences, the interest (`Int`) of each sentence's information, the degree (`Assim`) to which the information is taken to be assimilated by the user etc., as shown below. In INDIGO, comparisons are also marked up with angles that guide the robot to turn to the object(s) it compares to.

```
<Period>
  <Sentence Property=".../#type"
  Int="3" Assim="0">
    <Demonstrative ref=".../#exhibit1"
    role="owner">
      This</Demonstrative>
    <Verb>is</Verb>
    <NP ref=".../#Amphora" role="filler">
      an amphora</NP>
  </Sentence>
  <Punct>,</Punct>
  <Sentence Property=".../#subtype
  Int="3" Assim="1">
    <EmptyRef ref=".../#Amphora"
    role="owner"/>
    <NP ref=".../#Vessel" role="filler">
      a type of vessel</NP>
  </Sentence>
  <Punct>;</Punct>
  <Sentence Property=".../#paintedBy"
  Int="2" Assim="0">
    <Pronoun ref=".../#exhibit1"
    role="owner">
      it</Pronoun>
    <Verb>was painted</Verb>
    <Preposition>by</Preposition>
    <Name ref=".../#pKleo" role="filler">
      the painter of Kleophrades</Name>
  </Sentence>
  <Punct>.</Punct>
</Period>
```

2.1 Using NaturalOWL's Protégé plug-in

NaturalOWL's plug-in for Protégé can be used to specify all the linguistic and user modeling annotations of the ontologies that NaturalOWL requires. The annotations in effect establish a domain-dependent lexicon, whose entries are associated with classes or entities of the ontology; micro-plans, which are associated with properties of the ontology; a partial order of properties, which is used in document planning; interest scores, indicating how interesting the various facts of the ontology are to each user type; parameters that control, for example, the desired length of the generated texts. The plug-in can also be used to generate previews of the resulting texts, for different types of users, with or without comparisons, etc., as illustrated in figure 3. The resulting annotations are then saved in RDF.

2.2 Using NaturalOWL in Second Life

In Second Life, each user controls an avatar, which can, among other actions, move in the virtual world, touch objects, or communicate with other

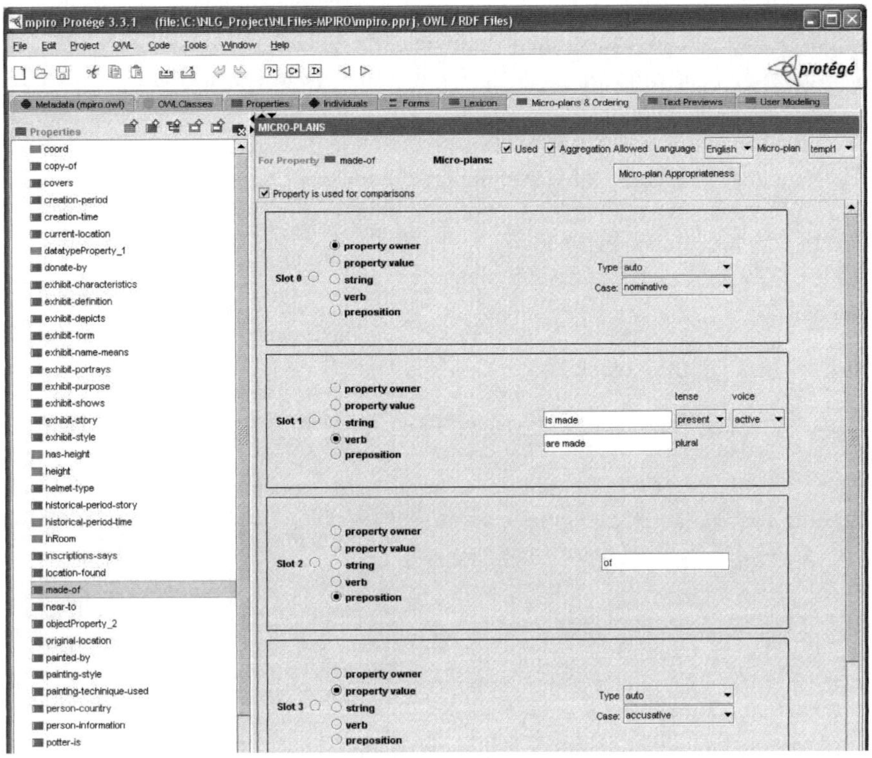

Figure 2: Specifying a micro-plan with NaturalOWL's Protégé plug-in.

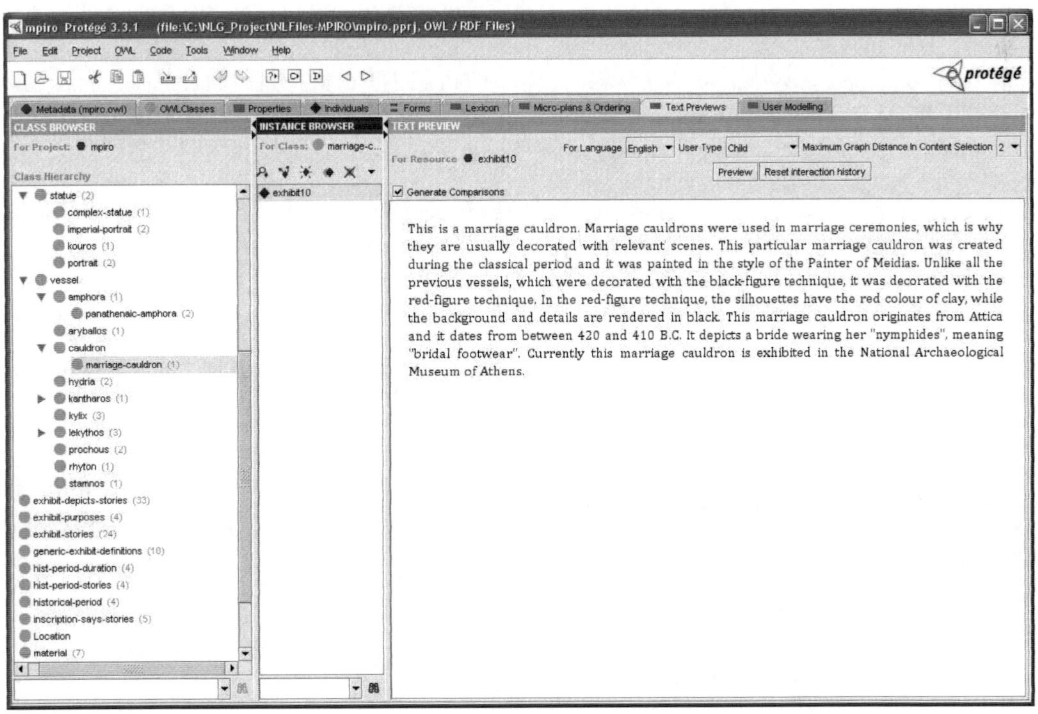

Figure 3: Generating a text preview with NaturalOWL's Protégé plug-in.

avatars; in the latter case, the user types text on the keyboard. In the Second Life application that we demonstrate, the robot is an avatar that is not controlled by a human, but by our own Second Life client software.[4] The client software includes a navigation component, which controls the robot's movement, and it allows the robot to "utter" texts generated by NaturalOWL, instead of expecting keyboard input. Whenever a visitor near the robot touches an exhibit, an appropriate event is sent to the robot, which then goes near the exhibit and starts describing it.[5]

3 Conclusions and further work

The demonstration presents an open-source natural language generation engine for OWL ontologies, which generates descriptions of entities and classes in English and Greek. The engine is accompanied by a Protégé plug-in, which can be used to annotate the ontologies with linguistic and user modeling information required by the generation engine. The demonstration includes an application in Second Life, where the generation engine is embedded in a robotic avatar acting as a museum guide. We are currently extending NaturalOWL to handle follow up questions about entities or classes mentioned in the generated texts.

Acknowledgments

NaturalOWL was developed in project XENIOS, which was funded by the Greek General Secretariat of Research and Technology and the European Union.[6] NaturalOWL is now being extended in project INDIGO, which is funded by the European Union; our work in INDIGO is also supported by additional funding from the Greek General Secretariat of Research and Technology.[7]

References

I. Androutsopoulos and D. Galanis. 2008. Generating natural language descriptions from OWL ontologies: experience from the NaturalOWL system. Technical report, Department of Informatics, Athens University of Economics and Business, Greece.

I. Androutsopoulos, J. Oberlander, and V. Karkaletsis. 2007. Source authoring for multilingual generation of personalised object descriptions. *Natural Language Engineering*, 13(3):191–233.

G. Antoniou and F. van Harmelen. 2004. *A Semantic Web primer*. MIT Press.

D. Bilidas, M. Theologou, and V. Karkaletsis. 2007. Enriching OWL ontologies with linguistic and user-related annotations: the ELEON system. In *Proceedings of the 19th IEEE International Conference on Tools with Artificial Intelligence*, Patras, Greece.

D. Galanis and I. Androutsopoulos. 2007. Generating multilingual descriptions from linguistically annotated OWL ontologies: the NATURALOWL system. In *Proceedings of the 11th European Workshop on Natural Language Generation*, pages 143–146, Schloss Dagstuhl, Germany.

A. Isard, J. Oberlander, I. Androutsopoulos, and C. Matheson. 2003. Speaking the users' languages. IEEE *Intelligent Systems*, 18(1):40–45.

S. Konstantopoulos, A. Tegos, D. Bilidas, I. Androutsopoulos, G. Lampouras, P. Malakasiotis, C. Matheson, and O. Deroo. 2009. Adaptive natural-language interaction. In *Proceedings of 12th Conference of the European Chapter of the Association for Computational Linguistics (system demonstrations)*, Athens, Greece.

J. Oberlander, G. Karakatsiotis, A. Isard, and I. Androutsopoulos. 2008. Building an adaptive museum gallery in Second Life. In *Proceedings of Museums and the Web*, Montreal, Quebec, Canada.

M. O'Donnell, C. Mellish, J. Oberlander, and A. Knott. 2001. ILEX: an architecture for a dynamic hypertext generation system. *Natural Language Engineering*, 7(3):225–250.

E. Reiter and R. Dale. 2000. *Building natural language generation systems*. Cambridge University Press.

D. Vogiatzis, D. Galanis, V. Karkaletsis, I. Androutsopoulos, and C.D. Spyropoulos. 2008. A conversant robotic guide to art collections. In *Proceedings of the 2nd Workshop on Language Technology for Cultural Heritage Data, Language Resources and Evaluation Conference*, Marrakech, Morocco.

[4]Our client was built using the `libsecondlife` library; see `http://www.libsecondlife.org/`. More precisely, the robot is an object controlled by an invisible robotic avatar, which is in turn controlled by our client.

[5]A video showing the robotic avatar in action is available at `http://www.vimeo.com/801099`.

[6]See `http://www.ics.forth.gr/xenios/`.

[7]See `http://www.ics.forth.gr/indigo/`.

eHumanities Desktop - An Online System for Corpus Management and Analysis in Support of Computing in the Humanities

Rüdiger Gleim[1], **Ulli Waltinger**[2], **Alexandra Ernst**[2], **Alexander Mehler**[1],
Tobias Feith[2] & Dietmar Esch[2]

[1]Goethe-Universität Frankfurt am Main, [2]Universität Bielefeld

Abstract

This paper introduces *eHumanities Desktop*- an online system for corpus management and analysis in support of Computing in the Humanities. Design issues and the overall architecture are described as well as an initial set of applications which are offered by the system.

1 Introduction

Since there is an ongoing shift towards computer based studies in the humanities new challenges in maintaining and analysing electronic resources arise. This is all the more because research groups are often distributed over several institutes and universities. Thus, the ability to collaboratively work on shared resources becomes an important issue. This aspect also marks a turn point in the development of Corpus Management Systems (CMS). Apart from the aspect of pure resource management, processing and analysis of documents have traditionally been the domain of desktop applications. Sometimes even to the point of command line tools. Therefore the technical skills needed to use for example linguistic tools have effectively constrained their usage by a larger community. We emphasise the approach to offer low-threshold access to both corpus management as well as processing and analysis in order to address a broader public in the humanities.

The *eHumanities Desktop*[1] is designed as a general purpose platform for scientists in humanities. Based on a sophisticated data model to manage authorities, resources and their interrelations the system offers an extensible set of application modules to process and analyse data. Users do not need to undertake any installation efforts but simply can login from any computer with internet connection using a standard browser. Figure 1 shows the desktop with the *Document Manager* and the *Administration Dialog* opened.

Figure 1: The eHumanities Desktop environment showing the document manager and administration dialog.

In the following we describe the general architecture of the system. The second part addresses an initial set of application modules which are currently available through *eHumanities Desktop*. The last section summarises the system description and gives a prospect of future work.

2 System Architecture

Figure 2 gives an overview of the general architecture. The *eHumanities Desktop* is implemented as a client/server system which can be used via any JavaScript/Java capable Web Browser. The GUI is based on the ExtJS Framework[2] and provides a look and feel similar to Windows Vista. The server side is based on Java Servlet technology using the Tomcat[3] Servlet Container. The core of the system is the *Command Dispatcher* which

[1]`http://hudesktop.hucompute.org`

[2]`http://extjs.com`

[3]`http://tomcat.apache.org`

Proceedings of the EACL 2009 Demonstrations Session, pages 21–24,
Athens, Greece, 3 April 2009. ©2009 Association for Computational Linguistics

manages the communication with the client and the execution of tasks like downloading a document for example. The *Master Data* include information about all objects managed by the system, for example users, groups, documents, resources and their interrelations. All this information is stored in a transactional Relational Database (using MySQL[4]). The underlying data model is described later in more detail. Another important component is the *Storage Handler*: Based on an automatic mime type[5] detection it decides how to store and retrieve documents. For example videos and audio material are best stored as files whereas XML documents are better accessible via a XML Database Management System or specialized DBMS (e.g. HyGraphDB (Gleim et al., 2007)). Which kind of *Storage Backend* is used to archive a given document is transparent to the user- and also to developers using the *Storage Handler*. The *Document Indexer* allows for structure sensitive indexing of text documents. That way a full text search can be realised. However this feature is not fully integrated at the moment and thus subject of future work. Finally the *Command Dispatcher* connects to an extensible set of application modules which allow to process and analyse stored documents. These are briefly introduced in the next section.

To get a better idea of how the described components work together we give an example of how the task to perform PoS tagging on a text document is accomplished: The task to process a specific document is sent from the client to the server. As a first step the *Command Dispatcher* checks based on the *Master Data* if the requesting user is logged in correctly, authorized to perform PoS tagging and has permission to read the document to be tagged. The next step is to fetch the document from the *Storage Handler* as input to the *PoS Tagger* application module. The tagger creates a new document which is handed over to the *Storage Handler* which decides how to store the resource. Since the output of the tagger is a XML document it is stored as a XML Database. Finally the information about the new document is stored in the *Master Data* including a reference to the original one in order to state from which document it has been derived. That way it is possible to track on which basis a given document has been created. Finally the *Command Dispatcher* signals the successful completion of the task back to the *Client*.

Figure 3 shows the class diagram of the master data model. The design is woven around the general concept that *authorities* have access permissions on *resources*. Authorities are distinguished into *users* and *groups*. Users can be members of one or more groups. Furthermore authorities can have permissions to use *features* of the system. That way it is possible to individually configure the spectrum of functions someone can effectively use. Resources are distinguished by *documents* and *repositories*. Repositories are containers, similar to directories known from file systems. An important addition is that resources can be member of an arbitrary number of repositories. That way a document or a repository can be used in different contexts allowing for easy corpus compilation.

A typical scenario which benefits from such a data model is a distributed research group consisting of several research teams: One team collects data from field research, a second processes and annotates the raw data and a third team performs statistical analysis. In this example every group has the need to share resources with others while keeping control over the data: The statistics team should be able to read the annotated data but must not be allowed to edit resources and so on.

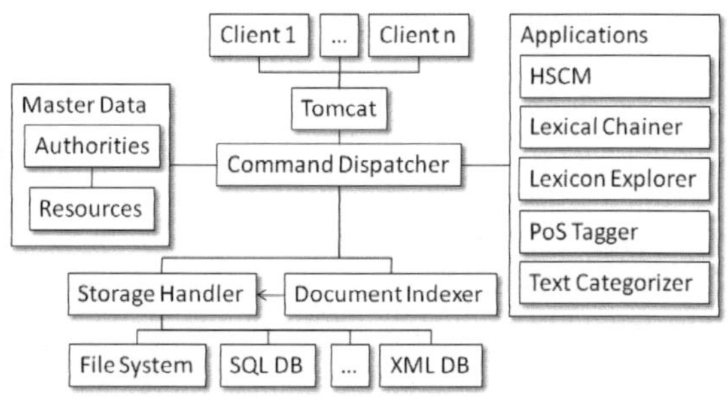

Figure 2: Overview of the System Architecture.

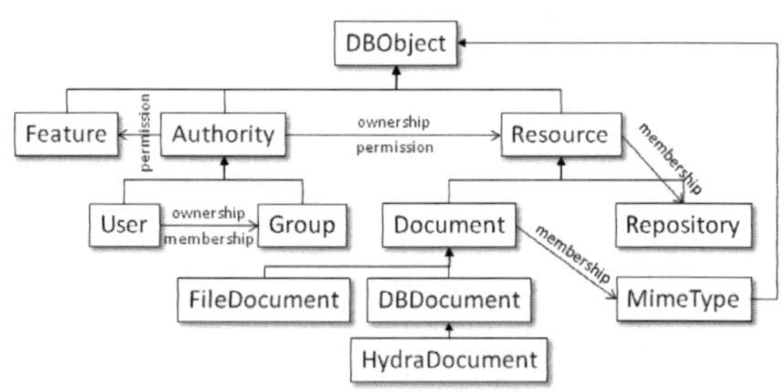

Figure 3: UML Class Diagram of the Master Data.

[4]http://dev.mysql.com

[5]http://www.iana.org/assignments/media-types/

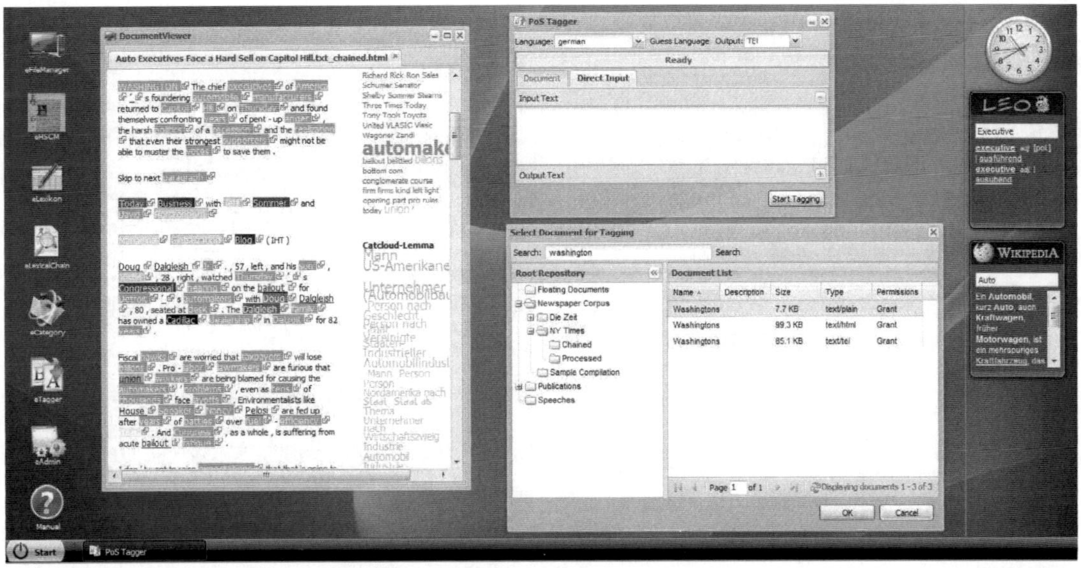

Figure 4: The eHumanities Desktop environment showing a chained document and the PoS Tagger dialog.

3 Applications

In the following we outline the initial set of applications which is currently available via *eHumanities Desktop*. Figure 4 gives an idea of the look and feel of the system. It shows the visualisation of a chained document and the PoS Tagger window with an opened document selection dialog.

3.1 Document Manager

The *Document Manager* is the core of the desktop. It allows to upload and download documents as well as sharing them with other users and groups. It follows the look and feel of the *Windows Explorer*. Documents and repositories can be created and edited via context menus. They can be moved via drag and drop between different repositories. Both can be copied via drag and drop while pressing the Ctrl-key. Note that repositories only contain references- so a copy is *not* a physical reduplication. Documents which are not assigned to any repository the current user can see are gathered in a special repository called *Floating Documents*. A double click on a file will open a document viewer which offers a rendered view of textual contents. The button 'Access Permissions' opens a dialog which allows to edit the rights of other users and groups on the currently selected resources. Finally a search dialog at the top makes documents searchable.

3.2 PoS Tagging

The PoS-Tagging module enables users to preprocess their uploaded documents. Besides tokenisation and sentence boundary detection, a trigram HMM-Tagger is implemented in the preprocessing system (Waltinger and Mehler, 2009). The tagging module was trained and evaluated based on the German Negra Corpus (Uszkoreit et al., 2006) (F-measure of 0.96) and the English Penn Treebank (Marcus et al., 1994) (F-measure of 0.956). Additionally a lemmatisation and stemming module is included for both languages. As an unifying exchange format the component utilises TEI P5 (Burnard, 2007).

3.3 Lexical Chaining

As a further linguistic application module a lexical chainer (Mehler, 2005; Mehler et al., 2007; Waltinger et al., 2008a; Waltinger et al., 2008b) has been included in the online desktop environment. That is, semantically related tokens of a given text can be tracked and connected by means of a lexical reference system. The system currently uses two different terminological ontologies - *WordNet* (Fellbaum, 1998) and *GermaNet* (Hamp and Feldweg, 1997) - as chaining resources which have been mapped onto the database format. However the list of resources for chaining can easily be extended.

3.4 Lexicon Exploration

With regards to lexicon exploration, the system aggregates different lexical resources including English, German and Latin. In this module, not only co-occurrence data, social and terminological ontologies but also social tagging enhanced data are available for a given input token.

3.5 Text Classification

An easy to use text classifier (Waltinger et al., 2008a) has been implemented into the system. In this, an automatic mapping of an unknown text onto a social ontology is enabled. The system uses the category tree of the German and English *Wikipedia-Project* in order to assign category information to textual data.

3.6 Historical Semantics Corpus Management

The HSCM is developed by the research project *Historical Semantics Corpus Management* (Jussen et al., 2007). The system aims at a texttechnological representation and quantitative analysis of chronologically layered corpora. It is possible to query for single terms or entire phrases. The contents can be accessed as rendered HTML as well as TEI P5[6] encoded. In its current state is supports to browse and analyse the *Patrologia Latina*[7].

4 Conclusion

This paper introduced *eHumanities Desktop*- a web based corpus management system which offers an extensible set of application modules which allow online exploration, processing and analysis of resources in humanities. The use of the system was exemplified by describing the Document Manager, PoS Tagging, Lexical Chaining, Lexicon Exploration, Text Classification and Historical Semantics Corpus Management. Future work will include flexible XML indexing and queries as well as full text search on documents. Furthermore the set of applications will be gradually extended.

References

Lou Burnard. 2007. New tricks from an old dog: An overview of tei p5. In Lou Burnard, Milena Dobreva, Norbert Fuhr, and Anke Lüdeling, editors, *Digital Historical Corpora- Architecture, Annotation, and Retrieval*, number 06491 in Dagstuhl Seminar Proceedings, Dagstuhl, Germany. Internationales Begegnungs- und Forschungszentrum für Informatik (IBFI), Schloss Dagstuhl, Germany.

Christiane Fellbaum, editor. 1998. *WordNet: An Electronic Lexical Database*. MIT Press, Cambridge.

Rüdiger Gleim, Alexander Mehler, and Hans-Jürgen Eikmeyer. 2007. Representing and maintaining large corpora. In *Proceedings of the Corpus Linguistics 2007 Conference, Birmingham (UK)*.

Birgit Hamp and Helmut Feldweg. 1997. Germanet - a lexical-semantic net for german. In *In Proceedings of ACL workshop Automatic Information Extraction and Building of Lexical Semantic Resources for NLP Applications*, pages 9–15.

Bernhard Jussen, Alexander Mehler, and Alexandra Ernst. 2007. A corpus management system for historical semantics. *Appears in: Sprache und Datenverarbeitung*.

Mitchell P. Marcus, Beatrice Santorini, and Mary A. Marcinkiewicz. 1994. Building a large annotated corpus of english: The penn treebank. *Computational Linguistics*, 19(2):313–330.

Alexander Mehler, Ulli Waltinger, and Armin Wegner. 2007. A formal text representation model based on lexical chaining. In *Proceedings of the KI 2007 Workshop on Learning from Non-Vectorial Data (LNVD 2007) September 10, Osnabrück*, pages 17–26, Osnabrück. Universität Osnabrück.

Alexander Mehler. 2005. Lexical chaining as a source of text chaining. In Jon Patrick and Christian Matthiessen, editors, *Proceedings of the 1st Computational Systemic Functional Grammar Conference, University of Sydney, Australia*, pages 12–21.

Hans Uszkoreit, Thorsten Brants, Sabine Brants, and Christine Foeldesi. 2006. Negra corpus.

Ulli Waltinger and Alexander Mehler. 2009. Web as preprocessed corpus: Building large annotated corpora from heterogeneous web document data. In preparation.

Ulli Waltinger, Alexander Mehler, and Gerhard Heyer. 2008a. Towards automatic content tagging: Enhanced web services in digital libraries using lexical chaining. In *4th Int. Conf. on Web Information Systems and Technologies (WEBIST '08), 4-7 May, Funchal, Portugal*. Barcelona.

Ulli Waltinger, Alexander Mehler, and Maik Stührenberg. 2008b. An integrated model of lexical chaining: Application, resources and its format. In Angelika Storrer, Alexander Geyken, Alexander Siebert, and Kay-Michael Würzner, editors, *Proceedings of KONVENS 2008 — Ergänzungsband Textressourcen und lexikalisches Wissen*, pages 59–70.

[6] http://www.tei-c.org/Guidelines/P5

[7] http://pld.chadwyck.co.uk/

A comparison of clausal coordinate ellipsis in Estonian and German: Remarkably similar elision rules allow a language-independent ellipsis-generation module

Karin Harbusch
Computer Science Department
University of Koblenz-Landau
Koblenz, Germany
harbusch@uni-koblenz.de

Mare Koit & Haldur Õim
Research Group of Computational Linguistics
University of Tartu
Tartu, Estonia
mare.koit@ut.ee & haldur.oim@ut.ee

Abstract

We compare the phenomena of clausal coordinate ellipsis in Estonian, a Finno-Ugric language, and German, an Indo-European language. The rules underlying these phenomena appear to be remarkably similar. Thus, the software module ELLEIPO, which was originally developed to generate clausal coordinate ellipsis in German and Dutch, works for Estonian as well. In order to extend ELLEIPO's coverage to Estonian, we only had to adapt the lexicon and some syntax rules unrelated to coordination. We describe the language-independent rules for coordinate ellipsis that ELLEIPO applies to non-elliptical syntactic structures in both target languages.

1 Introduction

In written German newspaper text, clausal coordination occurs in about 14% of the sentences, and coordinate ellipsis (e.g. (1)) in about 7% (see a corpus study by Harbusch and Kempen, 2007). Studies of ellipsis in Estonian are hardly available (cf. Erelt, 2003).

(1) *Monopole* ***sollen*** *geknackt* ~~***werden***~~ *und*
Monopolies should shattered be and
Märkte ~~***sollen***~~ *getrennt* ***werden***
markets should split be
'Monopolies should be shattered and markets split'

In order to deal with these relatively frequent phenomena, we develop an Estonian coordinate-ellipsis generator based on ELLEIPO, the software module written in JAVA that generates clausal coordinate ellipsis in German and Dutch (Harbusch and Kempen, 2006; 2009). Given the fact that the two target languages belong to two rather different language families (German is an Indo-European, Estonian a Finno-Ugric language) we expected the two target languages to differ considerably with respect to the rules for generating coordinate elisions; however, this expectation was falsified. As we will detail below, a pairwise comparison of a heterogeneous set of elliptical constructions in the target languages reveals that the German rules we had implemented in ELLEIPO also generate the Estonian structures. We only needed to adapt the lexicon and some syntax rules unrelated to coordination. The core algorithm worked language-independently for both languages.

The paper is organized as follows. In section 2, we first define the four main groups of clausal coordinate ellipsis phenomena, and show that the elisions in the two target languages obey basically the same rules. This implies that the Estonian version of the software system ELLEIPO can use the same core algorithm as the German and Dutch version. In section 3, we discuss other linguistic theories for clausal coordinate ellipsis, especially focussing on implementations for generation. In final section 4, we draw some conclusions and address options for future work.

2 Clause-level coordinate ellipsis in Estonian and German

In the literature, one often distinguishes four major types of clause-level coordinate ellipsis (which can become combined; cf. example (1)).[1]

- GAPPING, with three special variants called LONG DISTANCE GAPPING (LDG), SUBGAPPING, and STRIPPING,
- FORWARD CONJUNCTION REDUCTION (FCR),
- BACKWARD CONJUNCTION REDUCTION (BCR;

[1] We will not deal with the elliptical constructions known as VP Ellipsis, VP Anaphora and Pseudogapping because they involve the generation of pro-forms instead of, or in addition to, the ellipsis proper. For example, *John laughed, and Mary did, too*—a case of VP Ellipsis—includes the proform *did*. Nor do we deal with recasts of clausal coordinations as coordinate NPs (e.g., *John likes skating and Peter likes skiing* becoming *John and Peter like skating and skiing, respectively*). Presumably, such conversions involve a logical rather than syntactic mechanism.

Proceedings of the EACL 2009 Demonstrations Session, pages 25–28,
Athens, Greece, 3 April 2009. ©2009 Association for Computational Linguistics

also called *Right Node Raising*), and

- SUBJECT GAP IN CLAUSES WITH FINITE/ FRONTED VERBS (SGF).

They are illustrated in the English sentences (2) through (8). The subscripts denote the elliptical mechanism at work: *g* stands for Gapping, Subgapping, and Stripping, respectively; $g(g)^+$ is recursively added for LDG; *f* = FCR; *s* = SGF; *b* = BCR.

(2) GAPPING: *Jüri **lives** in Tallinn and his children* ~~***live***~~$_g$ *in Tartu*

(3) LDG: *My wife **wants to buy** a car and my son* ~~***wants***~~$_g$ *[~~**to buy**~~]*$_{gg}$ *a motorcycle*

(4) SUBGAPPING: *The driver **was** killed and the passengers* ~~***were***~~$_g$ *severely wounded*

(5) STRIPPING: *My sister **lives in Narva** and my brother **[~~lives in Narva~~]**$_g$ **too***

(6) FCR: *Pärnu is the city [S **where** Ainar lives and* ~~***where***~~$_f$ *Peeter works]*

(7) BCR: *Riina arrived before three **[~~o'clock~~]**$_b$ and Terje left after six **o'clock***

(8) SGF: *Into the wood went **the hunter** and **[~~the hunter~~]**$_s$ shot a hare*

In the theoretical framework by Kempen (2009) and its implementation for German and Dutch in ELLEIPO, the elision process is guided by constraints on *lemma-* and *wordform-identity* constraints and, to some extent, linear order.[2]

ELLEIPO's functioning is based on the assumption that coordinate ellipsis does not result from the application of declarative grammar rules for clause formation but from a procedural component that interacts with the sentence generator and may block the overt expression of certain constituents. Thus, the rules apply to assembled non-elliptical (unreduced) tree structures in the final stage of generation. Due to this feature, ELLEIPO can be combined, at least in principle, with various lexicalized-grammar formalisms. However, this advantage does not come entirely for free: The module needs a formalism-dependent interface that converts generator output to a *canonical form* consisting of "flat" syntactic trees where all major clause constituents are represented at the same hierarchical level (see Harbusch and Kempen 2006; 2007).

In the following, we introduce ELLEIPO's elision rules only in an informal manner (for the pseudocode of the algorithm, see Harbusch and Kempen, 2006; 2009). The rules described in the following can be applied in any order to unreduced syntactic structures in canonical form. In case of a successful rule application, the elidable constituents (and its non-elided counterpart in the other conjunct) is adorned with a subscript indicating the ellipsis type (as illustrated in (2) through (8)). ELLEIPO's final step executes all possible elliptical combinations (e.g., for example (1), it also realizes a version with Subgapping and LDG, respectively, i.e.: *Monopole **sollen** geknackt **werden** und Märkte* ~~***sollen***~~$_g$ *getrennt* ~~***werden***~~$_{gg}$).

In Gapping (see examples (9) and (10)), lemma-identical verbs can be elided from the second conjunct, if and only if a contrast is expressed, i.e. each remaining constituent in this conjunct has a counterpart with the same grammatical function in the first conjunct (cf. (11)).[3]

(9) *Mari **loeb** artikleid ja tema pojad* _$_g$ *pakse raamatuid*
*Mari **liest** Artikel und ihre Söhne* _$_g$ *dicke Bücher*
Mari reads articles and her sons thick books

(10) *Jüri **elab** Tartus ja Tallinnas* _$_g$ *tema pojad*
*Jüri **lebt** in Tartu und in Tallinn* _$_g$ *seine Söhne*
Jüri lives in Tartu and in Tallinn his sons

(11) **Mari **ostab** pirne ja Jüri* _$_g$ *turul*
Mari **kauft Birnen und Jüri* _$_g$ *auf dem Markt*
Mari buys pears and Jüri on the market

In *Long-Distance Gapping (LDG)*, the *remnants, i.e.* the non-elided constituents in the posterior conjunct, include constituents whose anterior counterparts belong to different clauses. *My wife* in (12) (translation of (3)) belongs to the main clause whereas *a car* is part of the infinitival complement clause. Notice that LDG does not require adjacency of the elided verbs (cf. the German example in (12)).

(12) *Minu naine **soovib osta** autot ja minu poeg* ~~***soovib***~~$_g$ ~~***osta***~~$_{gg}$ *mootorratast*
*Meine Frau **will** ein Auto **kaufen** und mein Sohn* ~~***will***~~$_g$ *ein Motorrad* ~~***kaufen***~~$_{gg}$

In *Subgapping*, the posterior conjunct includes a remnant in the form of a non-finite complement

[2] Coordinate structures consist of two or more *conjuncts* connected by a coordinating conjunction (in our examples: *and*). Rules of coordinate ellipsis license elision of some consituent in one conjunct under "identity" with a constituent in another conjunct. We distinguish between *lemma identity,* where only the word-stems of the constituents have to be identical, and *wordform identity,* which requires not only identity of the stems but also of their morphological features. Gapping only requires lemma identity (cf. examples (2) and (4)). In FCR, word-form identity is checked, i.e. the identical word string referring to the same referent (cf. *****The boy** loves dogs and **[~~the boys~~]**$_f$ hate cats*).

[3] For lack of space, here we cannot go into aspects of word-order variation (both Estonian and German are languages with relatively free word order). For the same reason, we only discuss examples with two conjuncts (although, ELLEIPO analyses *n*-ary coordinations as well), and cannot pay attention to coordinate structures that include negation.

clause ("VP"; *severely wounded* in (13); translation of (4)).

(13) *Juht* ***sai*** *surma ja reisijad* _$_g$ *tõsiselt vigastada*
Der Fahrer ***wurde*** *getötet und die Passagiere*
_$_g$ *ernsthaft verletzt*

Stripping is Gapping with the posterior conjunct consisting of one constituent only. This remnant is not a verb, and it is often supplemented by a modifier (such *too* in (14), the translation of (5)).

(14) *Mu õde* ***elab Narvas*** *ja mu vend* _$_g$ *samuti/ka.*
Meine Schwester ***lebt in Narva*** *und mein Bruder*
_$_g$ *ebenso/ auch*

In *Forward-Conjunction Reduction (FCR)*, a left-peripheral string of major constituents in the right conjunct is elided under wordform-identity with its counterpart in the right conjunct. In FCR example (15), the left-peripheral string comprising complementizer, subject and direct object are elided from the right-hand conjunct. If modifiers that are neither lemma- nor wordform-identical, are placed in between subject and object—as in (16)—, then elision of the object is blocked. (Actually, example (16) is not ill-formed but its right-hand conjunct cannot be interpreted as *cleaning the bike.*) In main-clause variant (17), elision of the direct object is blocked for similar reasons.

(15) ... ***et Jan oma jalgratta*** *asjatundlikult parandas*
... ***dass Jan sein Fahrrad*** *fachkundig reparierte*
... that Jan his bike expertly repaired
ja [~~et Jan oma jalgratta~~]$_f$ *hoolikalt puhastas*
und [~~dass Jan sein Fahrrad~~]$_f$ *eifrig putzte*
and that Jan his bike diligently cleaned

(16) *... ***et Jan*** *asjatundlikult* ***oma jalgratta*** *parandas*
... ***dass Jan*** *fachkundig* ***sein Fahrrad*** *reparierte*
ja [~~et Jan~~]$_f$ *hoolikalt* [~~oma jalgratta~~]$_f$ *puhastas*
und [~~dass Jan~~]$_f$ *eifrig* [~~sein Fahrrad~~]$_f$ *putzte*

(17) * ***Jan*** *parandas* ***oma jalgratta*** *asjatundlikult*
* ***Jan*** *reparierte* ***sein Fahrrad*** *fachkundig*
ja ~~Jan~~$_f$ *puhastas* [~~oma jalgratta~~]$_f$ *hoolikalt*
und ~~Jan~~$_f$ *putzte* [~~sein Fahrrad~~]$_f$ *eifrig*

Backward-Conjunction Reduction (BCR) licenses elision of a right-peripheral string in the left-hand conjunct under lemma-identity[4] with its counterpart in the right conjunct. However, unlike FCR's mirror image, BCR may cut into major constituents of the clause. In BCR example (18), the direct object can be elided in the first conjunct whereas in word-order variant (19), the verb blocks this elision. Example (20) illustrates that BCR, unlike the three other ellipsis types, may cut into major clausal constituents and only checks lemma-identity. Varying the objects to *'new bike'/'old bikes'*, and the second subject *'Peter'* to *'his brothers'* does not rule out ellipsis as long as peripheral access is guaranteed.

(18) *Jan parandas* [~~oma jalgratta~~]$_b$
Jan reparierte [~~sein Fahrrad~~]$_b$
Jan repaired his bike
ja Peeter puhastas ***oma jalgratta***
und Peter putzte ***sein Fahrrad***
and Peter cleaned his bike

(19) *... *et Jan* [~~oma jalgratta~~]$_b$ *parandas*
* ... *dass Jan* [~~sein Fahrrad~~]$_b$ *reparierte*
ja et Peeter ***oma jalgratta*** *puhastas*
und dass Peter ***sein Fahrrad*** *putzte*

(20) *Jan parandas* ***oma uue*** ~~jalgratta~~$_b$
Jan reparierte ***sein neues*** ~~Fahrrad~~$_b$
ja tema vennad puhastasid ***oma vanad jalgrattad***
und seine Brüder putzten ***ihre alten Fahrräder***

Examples (21)-(23) embody word-order variants within two simple coordinated clauses. The (il)licit elision patterns verify that in BCR the ellipsis should be right-peripheral in the left-hand conjunct, whereas in FCR the ellipsis is located left-peripherally in the right-hand conjunct.

(21) *Mari loeb* _$_b$ *ja Jüri kirjutab* ***raamatuid***
Mari liest _$_b$ *und Jüri schreibt* ***Bücher***
Mari reads and Jüri writes books

(22) *_$_b$ *Loeb Mari ja* ***raamatuid*** *kirjutab Jüri*
*_$_b$ *Liest Mari und* ***Bücher*** *schreibt Jüri*
reads Mari and books writes Jüri

(23) ***Raamatuid*** *loeb Mari ja* _$_f$ *kirjutab Jüri*
Bücher *liest Mari und* _$_f$ *schreibt Jüri*
Books reads Mari and writes Jüri

SGF (Subject Gap in clauses with Finite/Fronted verb) licenses elision of the subject of the right conjunct if in the left conjunct the subject follows the verb; however, the first constituent of the unreduced right-hand clausal conjunct must meet certain special requirements. In particular, it should be the subject of this clause (as in (24), translation of (8)) or a modifier (25), but not an argument other than the subject, e.g. neither complement nor (in)direct object (26). Additionally, if FCR is also possible, it should actually be realized in order to license SGF (for additional discussion of these restrictions, see Harbusch and Kempen, 2009).

(24) ***Metsa*** *läks* ***jahimees*** *ja* _$_s$ *tappis jänese*
In den Wald *ging* ***der Jäger*** *und* _$_s$ *schoss einen Hasen.*

(25) ***Miks/Eile*** *oled* ***sa*** *läinud ja*
Warum *bist* ***du*** *gegangen und*
Why have you left and
_$_f$ *ei ole* _$_s$ *midagi öelnud?*
_$_f$ *hast* _$_s$ *mich nicht gewarnt?*
have not me (Est.)/have me not (Ger.) warned
'Why did you leave but didn't you warn me?'

[4] ELLEIPO also checks case-identity to rule out *?Hilf* _$_{b[DAT]}$ *und reanimier [den Mann]*$_{ACC}$ 'Help and reanimate the man'

(26) ****Seda** **veini** *ei joo* **ma***
****Diesen Wein** trinke **ich** nicht*
This wine drink not I (Est.)/drink I not (Ger.)
enam ja ~~***[selle veini]***~~$_f$ *kallan* ~~***ma***~~$_s$ *ära*
mehr und ~~***[diesen Wein]***~~$_f$ *gieße* ~~***ich***~~$_s$ *weg*
anymore and this wine throw I away
'I don't drink this wine and throw it away'

Given the similarities between the rules that appear to control clausal coordinate ellipsis in German and Estonian, it is not surprising that the German/Dutch version of ELLEIPO could be tailored to Estonian easily. ELLEIPO's language-independent core algorithm generates Estonian ellipsis as well, as shown by the demonstrator. For the sake of completeness, we should add here that we have not been able to find types of clausal coordinate ellipsis in Estonian that go beyond the above four types; hence, as far as we can tell, Estonian does not require additional rules over and above those we needed for German and Dutch.

3 State of the art in ellipsis generation

All major grammar formalisms provide rules for clausal coordinate ellipsis—rules that tend to be intertwined with rules for nonelliptical coordination (e.g. Sarkar and Joshi (1996) for Tree Adjoining Grammar; Steedman (2000) for Combinatory Categorial Grammar; Frank (2002) for Functional Grammar; Crysman (2003) and Beavers and Sag (2004) for HPSG; and te Velde (2006) for the Minimalist Program). This also applies to many NLG systems (cf. Reiter and Dale, 2000). Generators that do include an autonomous component for coordinate ellipsis—that is, a component that takes unreduced coordinations expressed in the system's grammar formalism as input and return elliptical versions as output (Shaw, 1998; Dalianis, 1999; Hielkema, 2005)—use incomplete rule sets, thus risking over- or undergeneration, and incorrect or unnatural output.

4 Conclusion

Finally, we do not expect that the four types of clausal coordinate ellipsis presented here are "universal" in the sense that all natural languages exhibit all four of them and no language has additional types (see Harbusch and Kempen 2009 for some discussion based on language-typological work by Haspelmath, 2007). However, the experience described in this paper makes us confident that the "modular" approach taken in the ELLEIPO project will prove efficient when it comes to writing coordinate ellipsis rules for other languages—especially for languages belonging other language families.

References

John Beavers and Ivan A. Sag. 2004. Coordinate Ellipsis and Apparent Non-Constituent Coordination. In: *Procs. of 11th Int. HPSG Conf.*, Leuven, 48-69.

Hercules Dalianis. 1999. Aggregation in natural language generation. *Computational Intelligence, 15:* 384-414.

Berthold Crysmann. 2003. An asymmetric theory of peripheral sharing in HPSG. In: *Procs. of 8th Conf. on Formal Grammar*, Vienna.

Mati Erelt (Ed.). 2003. *Estonian Language.* Estonian Academy Publishers, Tallinn.

Anette Frank. 2002. A (discourse) functional analysis of asymmetric coordination. In*: Procs. of the LFG02 Conf.*, Athens, pp. 174-196.

Karin Harbusch and Gerard Kempen. 2006. ELLEIPO: A module that computes coordinate ellipsis for language generators that don't. In: *Procs. of 11th EACL,* Trento, pp. 115-118.

Karin Harbusch and Gerard Kempen. 2007. Clausal coordinate ellipsis in German. In: *Procs. of 16th NODALIDA*, Tartu, pp. 81-88.

Karin Harbusch and Gerard Kempen. 2009. Generating clausal coordinate ellipsis multilingually. In: *Procs. of 12th ENLG*, Athens.

Martin Haspelmath. 2007. Coordination. In: Timothy Shopen (Ed.), *Language typology and linguistic description.* Cambridge University Press, Cambridge, UK. [2nd Ed]

Feikje Hielkema. 2005. *Performing syntactic aggregation using discourse structures.* Unpublished Master's thesis, Artificial Intelligence Unit, University of Groningen.

Gerard Kempen. 2009. Clausal coordination and coordinate ellipsis in a model of the speaker. *Linguistics, 47(3).*

Ehud Reiter and Robert Dale. 2000. *Building natural language generation systems.* Cambridge University Press, Cambridge, UK.

Anoop Sarkar and Aravind Joshi. 1996. Coordination in Tree Adjoining Grammars: Formalization and implementation. In: *Procs. of 16th COLING,* Copenhagen, pp. 610–615.

James Shaw. 1998. Segregatory coordination and ellipsis in text generation. In: *Procs. of 17th COLING,* Montreal, pp. 1220-1226.

Mark Steedman. 2000. *The syntactic process.* MIT Press, Cambridge, MA.

John R. te Velde. 2006. *Deriving Coordinate Symmetries: A Phase-Based Approach Integrating Select, Merge, Copy and Match.* John Benjamins, Amsterdam.

Foma: a finite-state compiler and library

Mans Hulden
University of Arizona
mhulden@email.arizona.edu

Abstract

Foma is a compiler, programming language, and C library for constructing finite-state automata and transducers for various uses. It has specific support for many natural language processing applications such as producing morphological and phonological analyzers. Foma is largely compatible with the Xerox/PARC finite-state toolkit. It also embraces Unicode fully and supports various different formats for specifying regular expressions: the Xerox/PARC format, a Perl-like format, and a mathematical format that takes advantage of the 'Mathematical Operators' Unicode block.

1 Introduction

Foma is a finite-state compiler, programming language, and regular expression/finite-state library designed for multi-purpose use with explicit support for automata theoretic research, constructing lexical analyzers for programming languages, and building morphological/phonological analyzers, as well as spellchecking applications.

The compiler allows users to specify finite-state automata and transducers incrementally in a similar fashion to AT&T's fsm (Mohri et al., 1997) and Lextools (Sproat, 2003), the Xerox/PARC finite-state toolkit (Beesley and Karttunen, 2003) and the SFST toolkit (Schmid, 2005). One of Foma's design goals has been compatibility with the Xerox/PARC toolkit. Another goal has been to allow for the ability to work with n-tape automata and a formalism for expressing first-order logical constraints over regular languages and n-tape-transductions.

Foma is licensed under the GNU general public license: in keeping with traditions of free software, the distribution that includes the source code comes with a user manual and a library of examples.

The compiler and library are implemented in C and an API is available. The API is in many ways similar to the standard C library `<regex.h>`, and has similar calling conventions. However, all the low-level functions that operate directly on automata/transducers are also available (some 50+ functions), including regular expression primitives and extended functions as well as automata determinization and minimization algorithms. These may be useful for someone wanting to build a separate GUI or interface using just the existing low-level functions. The API also contains, mainly for spell-checking purposes, functionality for finding words that match most closely (but not exactly) a path in an automaton. This makes it straightforward to build spell-checkers from morphological transducers by simply extracting the range of the transduction and matching words approximately.

Unicode (UTF8) is fully supported and is in fact the only encoding accepted by Foma. It has been successfully compiled on Linux, Mac OS X, and Win32 operating systems, and is likely to be portable to other systems without much effort.

2 Basic Regular Expressions

Retaining backwards compatibility with Xerox/PARC and at the same time extending the formalism means that one is often able to construct finite-state networks in equivalent various ways, either through ASCII-based operators or through the Unicode-based extensions. For example, one can either say:

```
ContainsX = Σ⋆ X Σ⋆;
MyWords = {cat}|{dog}|{mouse};
MyRule = n -> m || _ p;
ShortWords = [MyLex¹]₁ ∩ Σ^<6;
```

or:

Proceedings of the EACL 2009 Demonstrations Session, pages 29–32,
Athens, Greece, 3 April 2009. ©2009 Association for Computational Linguistics

Operators	**Compatibility variant**	**Function**
[ ] ( )	[ ] ( )	grouping parentheses, optionality
∀ ∃	N/A	quantifiers
\ ‘		term negation, substitution/homomorphism
:	:	cross-product
+ ∗	+ ∗	Kleene closures
^<n ^>n ^{m,n}	^<n ^>n ^{m,n}	iterations
1 2	.1 .2 .u .l	domain & range
.f	N/A	eliminate all unification flags
¬ $ $. $?	~ $ $. $?	complement, containment operators
/ ./. /// \\\ /\/	/ ./. N/A N/A	‘ignores’, left quotient, right quotient, ‘inside’ quotient
∈ ∉ = ≠	N/A	language membership, position equivalence
≻ ≺	< >	precedes, follows
∨ ∪ ∧ ∩ - .P. .p.	$\mid$ & − .P. .p.	union, intersection, set minus, priority unions
=> -> (->) @->	=> -> (->) @->	context restriction, replacement rules
$\Vert$	<>	shuffle (asynchronous product)
× ∘	.x. .o.	cross-product, composition

Table 1: *The regular expressions available in Foma from highest to lower precedence. Horizontal lines separate precedence classes.*

```
define ContainsX ?* X ?*;
define MyWords {cat}|{dog}|{mouse};
define MyRule n -> m || _ p;
define ShortWords Mylex.i.l & ?^<6;
```

In addition to the basic regular expression operators shown in table 1, the formalism is extended in various ways. One such extension is the ability to use of a form of first-order logic to make existential statements over languages and transductions (Hulden, 2008). For instance, suppose we have defined an arbitrary regular language `L`, and want to further define a language that contains only one factor of `L`, we can do so by:

```
OneL = (∃x)(x ∈ L ∧ ¬(∃y)(y ∈ L
∧ ¬(x = y)));
```

Here, quantifiers apply to substrings, and we attribute the usual meaning to $\in$ and $\wedge$, and a kind of concatenative meaning to the predicate $S(t_1, t_2)$. Hence, in the above example, `OneL` defines the language where there exists a string x such that x is a member of the language L and there does not exist a string y, also in L, such that y would occur in a different position than x. This kind of logical specification of regular languages can be very useful for building some languages that would be quite cumbersome to express with other regular expression operators. In fact, many of the internally complex operations of Foma are built through a reduction to this type of logical expressions.

3 Building morphological analyzers

As mentioned, Foma supports reading and writing of the LEXC file format, where morphological categories are divided into so-called continuation classes. This practice stems back from the earliest two-level compilers (Karttunen et al., 1987). Below is a simple example of the format:

```
Multichar_Symbols +Pl +Sing
LEXICON Root
        Nouns;

LEXICON Nouns
cat     Plural;
church  Plural;

LEXICON Plural
+Pl:%^s        #;
+Sing          #;
```

4 An API example

The Foma API gives access to basic functions, such as constructing a finite-state machine from a regular expression provided as a string, performing a transduction, and exhaustively matching against a given string starting from every position.

The following basic snippet illustrates how to use the C API instead of the main interface of Foma to construct a finite-state machine encoding the language a^+b^+ and check whether a string matches it:

```
1. void check_word(char *s) {
2.   fsm_t *network;
3.   fsm_match_result *result;
4.
5.   network = fsm_regex("a+ b+");
6.   result = fsm_match(fsm, s);
7.   if (result->num_matches > 0)
8.     printf("Regex matches");
9.
10 }
```

Here, instead of calling the fsm_regex() function to construct the machine from a regular expressions, we could instead have accessed the beforementioned low-level routines and built the network entirely without regular expressions by combining low-level primitives, as follows, replacing line 5 in the above:

```
network = fsm_concat(
          fsm_kleene_plus(
          fsm_symbol("a")),
          fsm_kleene_plus(
          fsm_symbol("b")));
```

The API is currently under active development and future functionality is likely to include conversion of networks to 8-bit letter transducers/automata for maximum speed in regular expression matching and transduction.

5 Automata visualization and educational use

Foma has support for visualization of the machines it builds through the AT&T Graphviz library. For educational purposes and to illustrate automata construction methods, there is some support for changing the behavior of the algorithms.

For instance, by default, for efficiency reasons, Foma determinizes and minimizes automata between nearly every incremental operation. Operations such as unions of automata are also constructed by default with the product construction method that directly produces deterministic automata. However, this on-the-fly minimization and determinization can be relaxed, and a Thompson construction method chosen in the interface so that automata remain non-deterministic and non-minimized whenever possible—non-deterministic automata naturally being easier to inspect and analyze.

6 Efficiency

Though the main concern with Foma has not been that of efficiency, but of compatibility and extendibility, from a usefulness perspective it is important to avoid bottlenecks in the underlying algorithms that can cause compilation times to skyrocket, especially when constructing and combining large lexical transducers. With this in mind, some care has been taken to attempt to optimize the underlying primitive algorithms. Table 2 shows a comparison with some existing toolkits that build deterministic, minimized automata/transducers. One the whole, Foma seems to perform particularly well with pathological cases that involve exponential growth in the number of states when determinizing non-deterministic machines. For general usage patterns, this advantage is not quite as dramatic, and for average use Foma seems to perform comparably with e.g. the Xerox/PARC toolkit, perhaps with the exception of certain types of very large lexicon descriptions (>100,000 words).

7 Conclusion

The Foma project is multipurpose multi-mode finite-state compiler geared toward practical construction of large-scale finite-state machines such as may be needed in natural language processing as well as providing a framework for research in finite-state automata. Several wide-coverage morphological analyzers specified in the LEXC/xfst format have been compiled successfully with Foma. Foma is free software and will remain under the GNU General Public License. As the source code is available, collaboration is encouraged.

	Foma	xfst	GNU flex	AT&T fsm 4
$\Sigma^* a \Sigma^{15}$	0.216s	16.23s	17.17s	1.884s
$\Sigma^* a \Sigma^{20}$	8.605s	nf	nf	153.7s
North_Sami	14.23s	4.264s	N/A	N/A
8queens	0.188s	1.200s	N/A	N/A
sudoku2x3	5.040s	5.232s	N/A	N/A
lexicon.lex	1.224s	1.428s	N/A	N/A
3sat30	0.572s	0.648s	N/A	N/A

Table 2: *A relative comparison of running a selection of regular expressions and scripts against other finite-state toolkits. The first and second entries are short regular expressions that exhibit exponential behavior. The second results in a FSM with 2^{21} states and 2^{22} arcs. The others are scripts that can be run on both Xerox/PARC and Foma. The file lexicon.lex is a LEXC format English dictionary with 38418 entries. North_Sami is a large lexicon (lexc file) for the North Sami language available from* `http://divvun.no`.

References

Beesley, K. and Karttunen, L. (2003). *Finite-State Morphology*. CSLI, Stanford.

Hulden, M. (2008). Regular expressions and predicate logic in finite-state language processing. In Piskorski, J., Watson, B., and Yli-Jyrä, A., editors, *Proceedings of FSMNLP 2008*.

Karttunen, L., Koskenniemi, K., and Kaplan, R. M. (1987). A compiler for two-level phonological rules. In Dalrymple, M., Kaplan, R., Karttunen, L., Koskenniemi, K., Shaio, S., and Wescoat, M., editors, *Tools for Morphological Analysis*. CSLI, Palo Alto, CA.

Mohri, M., Pereira, F., Riley, M., and Allauzen, C. (1997). AT&T FSM Library-Finite State Machine Library. *AT&T Labs—Research*.

Schmid, H. (2005). A programming language for finite-state transducers. In Yli-Jyrä, A., Karttunen, L., and Karhumäki, J., editors, *Finite-State Methods and Natural Language Processing FSMNLP 2005*.

Sproat, R. (2003). Lextools: a toolkit for finite-state linguistic analysis. *AT&T Labs—Research*.

The Software Architecture for the First Challenge on Generating Instructions in Virtual Environments

Alexander Koller
Saarland University
koller@mmci.uni-saarland.de

Donna Byron
Northeastern University
dbyron@ccs.neu.edu

Justine Cassell
Northwestern University
justine@northwestern.edu

Robert Dale
Macquarie University
Robert.Dale@mq.edu.au

Johanna Moore
University of Edinburgh
J.Moore@ed.ac.uk

Jon Oberlander
University of Edinburgh
J.Oberlander@ed.ac.uk

Kristina Striegnitz
Union College
striegnk@union.edu

Abstract

The GIVE Challenge is a new Internet-based evaluation effort for natural language generation systems. In this paper, we motivate and describe the software infrastructure that we developed to support this challenge.

1 Introduction

Natural language generation (NLG) systems are notoriously hard to evaluate. On the one hand, simply comparing system outputs to a gold standard is not appropriate because there can be multiple generated outputs that are equally good, and finding metrics that account for this variability and produce results consistent with human judgments and task performance measures is difficult (Belz and Gatt, 2008; Stent et al., 2005; Foster, 2008). On the other hand, lab-based evaluations with human subjects to assess each aspect of the system's functionality are expensive and time-consuming. These characteristics make it hard to compare different systems and measure progress.

GIVE ("Generating Instructions in Virtual Environments") (Koller et al., 2007) is a research challenge for the NLG community designed to provide a new approach to NLG system evaluation. In the GIVE scenario, users try to solve a treasure hunt in a virtual 3D world that they have not seen before. The computer has a complete symbolic representation of the virtual environment. The challenge for the NLG system is to generate, in real time, natural-language instructions that will guide the users to the successful completion of their task (see Fig. 1). One crucial advantage of this generation task is that the NLG system and the user can be physically separated. This makes it possible to carry out a task-based evaluation over the Internet – an approach that has been shown to provide generous amounts of data in earlier studies (von Ahn and Dabbish, 2004; Orkin and Roy, 2007).

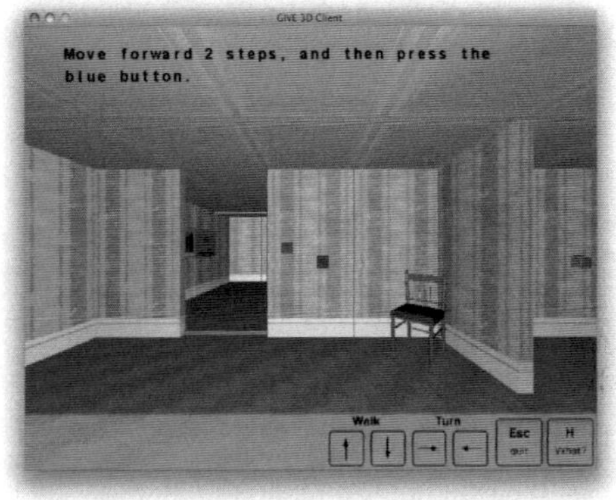

Figure 1: The GIVE Challenge.

In this paper, we describe the software architecture underlying the GIVE Challenge. The software connects each player in a 3D game world with an NLG system over the Internet. It is implemented and open source, and can be a used online during EACL at www.give-challenge.org. In Section 2, we give an introduction to the GIVE evaluation methodology by describing the experience of a user participating in the evaluation, the nature of the data we collect, and our scientific goals. Then we explain the software architecture behind the scenes and sketch the API that concrete NLG systems must implement in Section 3. In Section 4, we present some preliminary evaluation results, before we conclude in Section 5.

2 Evaluation method

Users participating in the GIVE evaluation start the 3D game from our website at www.give-challenge.org. They then see a 3D game window as in Fig. 1, which displays instructions and allows them to move around in the world and manipulate objects. The first room is a tutorial room where users learn how to interact with

Proceedings of the EACL 2009 Demonstrations Session, pages 33–36,
Athens, Greece, 3 April 2009. ©2009 Association for Computational Linguistics

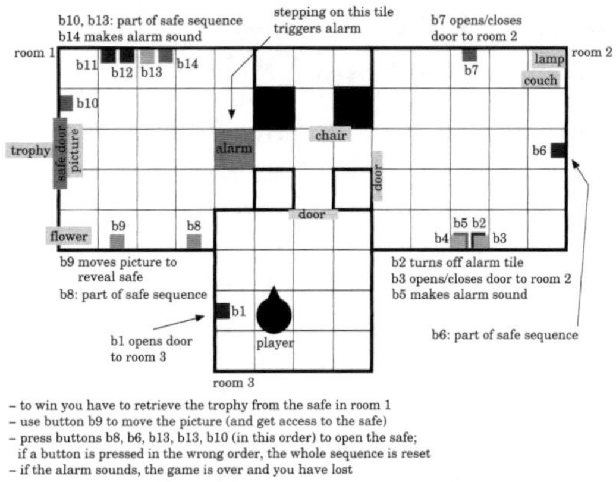

Figure 2: The map of a virtual world.

the system; they then enter one of three evaluation worlds, where instructions for solving the treasure hunt are generated by an NLG system.

The map of one of the game worlds is shown in Fig. 2: In this world, players must pick up a trophy, which is in a wall safe behind a picture. In order to access the trophy, they must first push a button to move the picture to the side, and then push another sequence of buttons to open the safe. One floor tile is alarmed, and players lose the game if they step on this tile without deactivating the alarm first. There are also a number of distractor buttons which either do nothing when pressed or set off an alarm. These distractor buttons are intended to make the game harder and, more importantly, to require appropriate reference to objects in the game world. Finally, game worlds can contain a number of objects such as chairs and flowers which are irrelevant for the task, but can be used as landmarks by a generation system.

Users are asked to fill out a before- and after-game questionnaire that collects some demographic data and asks the user to rate various aspects of the instructions they received. Every action that players take in a game world, and every instruction that a generation system generates for them, is recorded in a database. In addition to the questionnaire data, we are thus able to compute a number of objective measures such as:

- the percentage of users each system leads to a successful completion of the task;
- the average time, the average number of instructions, and the average number of in-game actions that this success requires;
- the percentage of generated referring expressions that the user resolves correctly; and
- average reaction times to instructions.

It is important to note that we have designed the GIVE Challenge not as a competition, but as a friendly evaluation effort where people try to learn from each other's successes. This is reflected in the evaluation measures above, which are in tension with one another: For instance, a system which gives very low-level instructions ("move forward"; "ok, now move forward"; "ok, now turn left") will enjoy short reaction times, but it will require more instructions than a system that aggregates these. To further emphasize this perspective, we will also provide a number of diagnostic tools, such as heat maps that show how much time users spent on each tile, or a playback function which displays an entire game run in real time.

In summary, the GIVE Challenge is a novel evaluation effort for NLG systems. It is motivated by real applications (such as pedestrian navigation and the generation of task instructions), makes no assumptions about the internal structure of an NLG system, and emphasizes the *situated* generation of discourse in a simulated physical environment. The game world is scalable; it can be made more complex and it can be adapted to focus on specific issues in natural language generation.

3 Architecture

A crucial aspect of the GIVE evaluation methodology is that it physically separates the user and the NLG system and connects them over the Internet. To achieve this, the GIVE software infrastructure consists of three components:

1. the *client*, which displays the 3D world to users and allows them to interact with it;
2. the *NLG servers*, which generate the natural-language instructions; and
3. the *Matchmaker*, which establishes connections between clients and NLG servers.

These three components run on different machines. The client is downloaded by users from our website and run on their local machine; each NLG server is run on a server at the institution that implemented it; and the Matchmaker runs on a central server we provide.

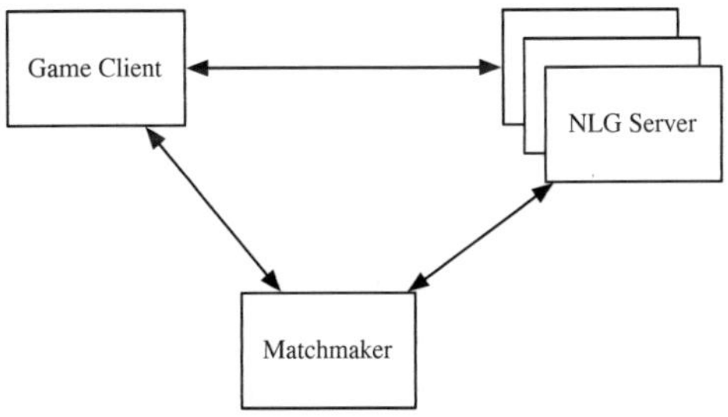

Figure 3: The GIVE architecture.

```
abstract class NlgSystem:
    void connectionEstablished();
    void connectionDisconnected();
    void handleStatusInformation(Position playerPosition,
                                 Orientation playerOrientation,
                                 List⟨String⟩ visibleObjects);
    void handleAction(Atom actionInstance,
                      List⟨Formula⟩ updates);
    void handleDidNotUnderstand();
    void handleMoveTurnAction(Direction direction);
    ...
```

Figure 4: The interface of an NLG system.

When a user starts the client, it connects over the Internet to the Matchmaker. The Matchmaker then selects a game world and an NLG server at random, and requests the NLG server to spawn a new *server instance*. It then sends the game world to the client and the server instance and disconnects from them, ready to handle new connections from other clients. The client and the server instance play one game together: Whenever the user does something, the client sends a message about this to the server instance, and the server instance can also send a message back to the client at any time, which will then be displayed as an instruction. When the game ends, the client and the server instance disconnect from each other. The server instance sends a log of all game events to the Matchmaker, and the client sends the questionnaire results to the Matchmaker; these then are stored in the database for later analysis.

All of these components are implemented in Java. This allows the client to be portable across all major operating systems, and to be started directly from the website via Java Web Start without the need for software installation. We felt it was important to make startup of the client as effortless as possible, in order to maximize the number of users willing to play the game. Unsurprisingly, we had to spend the majority of the programming time on the 3D graphics (based on the free jMonkeyEngine library) and the networking code. We could have reduced the effort required for these programming tasks by building upon an existing virtual 3D world system such as Second Life. However, we judged that the effort needed to adapt such a system to our needs would have been at least as high (in particular, we would have had to ensure that the user could only move according to the rules of the GIVE game and to instrument the virtual world to obtain real-time updates about events), and the result would have been less extensible to future installments of the challenge.

Since we provided all the 3D, networking, and database code, the research teams being evaluated were able to concentrate on the development of their NLG systems. Our only requirement was that they implement a concrete subclass of the class `NlgSystem`, shown in Fig. 4. This involves overriding the six abstract callback methods in this class with concrete implementations in which the NLG system reacts to specific events. The methods `connectionEstablished` and `connectionDisconnected` are called when users enter the game world and when they disconnect from the game. The method `handleAction` gets called whenever the user performs some physical action, such as pushing a button, and specifies what changed in the world due to this action; `handleMoveTurnAction` gets called whenever the user moves; `handleDidNotUnderstand` gets called whenever users press the H key to signal that they didn't understand the previous instruction; and `handleStatusInformation` gets called once per second and after each user action to inform the server of the player's position and orientation and the visible objects. Ultimately, each of these method calls gets triggered by a message that the client sends over the network in reaction to some event; but this is completely hidden from the NLG system developer.

The NLG system can use the method `send` to send a string to the client to be displayed. It also has access to various methods querying the state of the game world and to an interface to an external planner which can compute a sequence of actions leading to the goal.

4 First results

For this first installment of the GIVE Challenge, four research teams from the US, the Netherlands, and Spain provided generation systems, and a number of other research groups expressed their interest in participating, but weren't able to participate due to time constraints. Given that this was the first time we organized this task, we find this a very encouraging number. All four of the teams consisted primarily of students who implemented the NLG systems over the Northern-hemisphere summer. This is in line with our goal of taking this first iteration as a "dry run" in which we could fine-tune the software, learn about the easy and hard aspects of the challenge, and validate the evaluation methodology.

Public involvement in the GIVE Challenge was launched with a press release in early November 2008; the Matchmaker and the NLG servers were then kept running until late January 2009. During this time, online users played over 1100 games, which translates into roughly 75 game runs for each experimental condition (i.e., five different NLG systems paired with three different game worlds). To our knowledge, this makes GIVE the largest NLG evaluation effort yet in terms of experimental subjects.

While we have not yet carried out the detailed evaluation, the preliminary results look promising: a casual inspection shows that there are considerable differences in task success rate among the different systems.

While there is growing evidence from different research areas that the results of Internet-based evaluations are consistent with more traditional lab-based experiments (e.g., (Keller et al., 2008; Gosling et al., 2004)), the issue is not yet settled. Therefore, we are currently conducting a lab-based evaluation of the GIVE NLG systems, and will compare those results to the qualitative and quantitative data provided by the online subjects.

5 Conclusion

In this paper, we have sketched the GIVE Challenge and the software infrastructure we have developed for it. The GIVE Challenge is, to the best of our knowledge, the largest-scale NLG evaluation effort with human experimental subjects. This is made possible by connecting users and NLG systems over the Internet; we collect evaluation data automatically and unobtrusively while the user simply plays a 3D game. While we will report on the results of the evaluation in more detail at a later time, first results seem encouraging in that the performance of different NLG systems differs considerably.

In the future, we will extend the GIVE Challenge to harder tasks. Possibilities includ making GIVE into a dialogue challenge by allowing the user to speak as well as act in the world; running the challenge in a continuous world rather than a world that only allows discrete movements; or making it multimodal by allowing the NLG system to generate arrows or virtual human gestures. All these changes would only require limited changes to the GIVE software architecture. However, the exact nature of future directions remains to be discussed with the community.

References

A. Belz and A. Gatt. 2008. Intrinsic vs. extrinsic evaluation measures for referring expression generation. In *Proceedings of ACL-08:HLT, Short Papers*, pages 197–200, Columbus, Ohio.

M. E. Foster. 2008. Automated metrics that agree with human judgements on generated output for an embodied conversational agent. In *Proceedings of INLG 2008*, pages 95–103, Salt Fork, OH.

S. D. Gosling, S. Vazire, S. Srivastava, and O. P. John. 2004. Should we trust Web-based studies? A comparative analysis of six preconceptions about Internet questionnaires. *American Psychologist*, 59:93–104.

F. Keller, S. Gunasekharan, N. Mayo, and M. Corley. 2008. Timing accuracy of web experiments: A case study using the WebExp software package. *Behavior Research Methods*, to appear.

A. Koller, J. Moore, B. di Eugenio, J. Lester, L. Stoia, D. Byron, J. Oberlander, and K. Striegnitz. 2007. Shared task proposal: Instruction giving in virtual worlds. In M. White and R. Dale, editors, *Working group reports of the Workshop on Shared Tasks and Comparative Evaluation in Natural Language Generation*. Available at `http://www.ling.ohio-state.edu/nlgeval07/report.html`.

J. Orkin and D. Roy. 2007. The restaurant game: Learning social behavior and language from thousands of players online. *Journal of Game Development*, 3(1):39–60.

A. Stent, M. Marge, and M. Singhai. 2005. Evaluating evaluation methods for generation in the presence of variation. In *Proceedings of CICLing 2005*.

L. von Ahn and L. Dabbish. 2004. Labeling images with a computer game. In *Proceedings of the ACM CHI Conference*.

Adaptive Natural Language Interaction

Stasinos Konstantopoulos
Athanasios Tegos
Dimitris Bilidas
NCSR 'Demokritos', Athens, Greece

Ion Androutsopoulos
Gerasimos Lampouras
Prodromos Malakasiotis
Athens Univ. of Economics and Business
Greece

Colin Matheson
Human Communication Research Centre
Edinburgh University, U.K.

Olivier Deroo
Acapela Group, Belgium

Abstract

The subject of this demonstration is natural language interaction, focusing on adaptivity and profiling of the dialogue management and the generated output (text and speech). These are demonstrated in a museum guide use-case, operating in a simulated environment. The main technical innovations presented are the profiling model, the dialogue and action management system, and the text generation and speech synthesis systems.

1 Introduction

In this demonstration we present a number of state-of-the art language technology tools, implementing and integrating the latest discourse and knowledge representation theories into a complete application suite, including:

- dialogue management, natural language generation, and speech synthesis, all modulated by a flexible and highly adaptable profiling mechanism;
- robust speech recognition and language interpretation; and,
- an authoring environment for developing the representation of the domain of discourse as well as the associated linguistic and adaptivity resources.

The system demonstration is based on a use case of a virtual-tour guide in a museum domain. Demonstration visitors interact with the guide using headsets and are able to experiment with loading different interaction profiles and observing the differences in the guide's behaviour. The demonstration also includes the screening of videos from an embodied instantiation of the system as a robot guiding visitors in a museum.

2 Technical Content

The demonstration integrates a number of state-of-the-art language components into a highly adaptive natural language interaction system. Adaptivity here refers to using *interaction profiles* that modulate dialogue management as well as text generation and speech synthesis. Interaction profiles are semantic models that extend the objective ontological model of the domain of discourse with subjective information, such as how 'interesting' or 'important' an entity or statement of the objective domain model is.

Advanced *multimodal dialogue management* capabilities involving and combining input and output from various interaction modalities and technologies, such as speech recognition and synthesis, natural language interpretation and generation, and recognition of/response to user actions, gestures, and facial expressions.

State-of-the art *natural language generation* technology, capable of producing multi-sentence, coherent natural language descriptions of objects based on their abstract semantic representation. The resulting descriptions vary dynamically in terms of content as well as surface language expressions used to realize each description, depending on the interaction history (e.g., comparing to previously given information) and the adaptivity parameters (exhibiting system personality and adapting to user background and interests).

3 System Description

The system is capable of interacting in a variety of modalities, including non-verbal ones such as gesture and face-expression recognition, but in this demonstration we focus on the system's language interaction components. In this modality, abstract, language-independent system actions are first planned by the *dialogue and action manager* (DAM), then realized into language-specific text

Proceedings of the EACL 2009 Demonstrations Session, pages 37–40,
Athens, Greece, 3 April 2009.

by the *natural language generation engine*, and finally *synthesized* into speech. All three layers are parametrized by a *profiling and adaptivity* module.

3.1 Profiling and Adaptation

Profiling and adaptation modulates the output of dialogue management, generation, and speech synthesis so that the system exhibits a synthetic personality, while at the same time adapting to user background and interests.

User stereotypes (e.g., 'expert' or 'child') provide generation parameters (such as maximum description length) and also initialize the dynamic user model with *interest rates* for all the ontological entities (individuals and properties) of the domain of discourse. This same information is also provided in *system profiles* reflecting the system's (as opposed to the users') preferences; one can, for example, define a profile that favours using the architectural attributes to describe a building where another profile would choose to concentrate on historical facts regarding the same building.

Stereotypes and profiles are combined into a single set of parameters by means of *personality models*. Personality models are many-valued Description Logic definitions of the overall preference, grounded in stereotype and profile data. These definitions model recognizable personality traits so that, for example, an open personality will attend more to the user's requests than its own interests in deriving overall preference (Konstantopoulos et al., 2008).

Furthermore, the system *dynamically* adapts overall preference according to both interaction history and the current dialogue state. So, for one, the initial (static model) interest factor of an ontology entity is reduced each time this entity is used in a description in order to avoid repetitions. On the other hand, preference will increase if, for example, in the current state the user has explicitly asked about an entity.

3.2 Dialogue and Action Management

The DAM is built around the information-state update dialogue paradigm of the TRINDIKIT dialogue-engine toolkit (Cooper and Larsson, 1998) and takes into account the combined user-robot interest factor when determining information state updates.

The DAM combines various interaction modalities and technologies in both interpretation/fusion and generation/fission. In interpreting user actions the system recognizes spoken utterances, simple gestures, and touch-screen input, all of which may be combined into a representation of a multi-modal user action. Similarly, when planning robotic actions the DAM coordinates a number of available output modalities, including spoken language, text (on the touchscreen), the movement and configuration of the robotic platform, facial expressions, and simple head gestures.[1]

To handle multimodal input, the DAM uses a fusion module which combines messages from the language interpretation, gesture, and touchscreen modules into a single XML structure. Schematically, this can be represented as:

```
<userAction>
  <userUtterance>hello</userUtterance>
  <userButton content="13"/>
</userAction>
```

This structure represents a user pressing something on the touchscreen and saying *hello* at the same time.[2]

The representation is passed essentially unchanged to the DAM, to be processed by its update rules, where the ID of button press is interpreted in context and matched with the speech. In most circumstances, the natural language processing component (see 3.3) produces a semantic representation of the input which appears in the `userUtterance` element; the use of 'hello' above is for illustration. An example update rule which will fire in the context of a greeting from the user is (in schematic form):

```
if
 in(/latest_utterance/moves,  hello)
then
 output(start)
```

Update rules contain a list of conditions and a list of effects. Here there is one condition (that the latest moves from the user includes 'hello'), and one effect (the 'start' procedure). The latter initiates the dialogue by, among other things, having the system utter a standardised greeting.

As noted above, the DAM is also multimodal on the output side. An XML representation is created which can contain robot utterances and robot movements (both head movements and mobile platform moves). Information can also be presented on the touchscreen.

[1]Expressions and gestures will not be demonstrated, as they can not be materialized in the simulated robot.

[2]The precise meaning of 'at the same time' is determined by the fusion module.

3.3 Natural Language Processing

The NATURALOWL natural language generation (NLG) engine (Galanis et al, 2009) produces multi-sentence, coherent natural language descriptions of objects in multiple languages from a single semantic representation; the resulting descriptions are annotated with prosodic markup for driving the speech synthesisers.

The generated descriptions vary dynamically, in both content and language expressions, depending on the interaction profile as well as the dynamic interaction history. The dynamic preference factor of the item itself is used to decide the level of detail of the description being generated. The preference factors of the properties are used to order the contents of the descriptions to ensure that, in cases where not all possible facts are to be presented in a single turn, the most relevant ones are chosen. The interaction history is used to check previously given information to avoid repeating the same information in different contexts and to create comparisons with earlier objects.

NaturalOWL demonstrates the benefits of adopting NLG on the Semantic Web. Organizations that need to publish information about objects, such as exhibits or products, can publish OWL ontologies instead of texts. NLG engines, embedded in browsers or Web servers, can then render the ontologies in natural language, whereas computer programs may access the ontologies, in effect logical statements, directly. The descriptions can be very simple and brief, relying on question answering to provide more information if such is requested. This way, machine-readable information can be more naturally inspected and consulted by users.

In order to generate a list of possible follow up questions that the system can handle, we initially construct a list of the particular individuals or classes that are mentioned in the generated description; the follow up questions will most likely refer to them. Only individuals and classes for which there is further information in the ontology are extracted.

After identifying the referred individuals and classes, we proceed to predict definition (e.g., 'Who was Ares?') and property questions (e.g., 'Where is Mount Penteli?') about them that could be answered by the information in the ontology. We avoid generating questions that cannot be answered. The expected definition questions are constructed by inserting the names of the referred individuals and classes into templates such as 'who is/was *person X*?' or 'what do you know about *class or entity Y*?'.

In the case of referred individuals, we also generate expected property questions using the patterns NaturalOWL generates the descriptions with. These patterns, called *microplans*, show how to express the properties of the ontology as sentences of the target languages. For example, if the individual templeOfAres has the property excavatedIn, and that property has a microplan of the form '*resource* was excavated in *period*', we anticipate questions such as 'when was the Temple of Ares excavated?' and 'which period was the Temple of Ares excavated in?'.

Whenever a description (e.g., of a monument) is generated, the expected follow up questions for that description (e.g., about the monument's architect) are dynamically included in the rules of the speech recognizer's grammar, to increase word recognition accuracy. The rules include components that extract entities, classes, and properties from the recognized questions, thus allowing the dialogue and action manager to figure out what the user wishes to know.

3.4 Speech Synthesis and Recognition

The natural language interface demonstrates robust speech recognition technology, capable of recognizing spoken phrases in noisy environments, and advanced speech synthesis, capable of producing spoken output of very high quality. The main challenge that the *automatic speech recognition* (ASR) module needs to address is background noise, especially in the robot-embodied use case. A common technique used in order to handle this is training acoustic models with the anticipated background noise, but that is not always possible. The demonstrated ASR module can be trained on noise-contaminated data where available, but also incorporates *multi-band acoustic modelling* (Dupont, 2003) for robust recognition under noisy conditions. Speech recognition rates are also substantially improved by using the predictions made by NATURALOWL and the DAM to dynamically restrict the lexical and phrasal expectations at each dialogue turn.

The *speech synthesis* module of the demonstrated system is based on *unit selection technology*, generally recognized as producing more natural output that previous technologies such as diphone concatenation or formant synthesis. The main innovation that is demonstrated is support for emotion, a key aspect of increasing the naturalness of synthetic speech. This is achieved by combining emotional unit recordings with run-time transformations. With respect to the former, a complete 'voice' now comprises three sub-voices (*neutral*, *happy*, and *sad*), based on recordings of the same speaker. The recording time needed is substantially decreased by prior linguistic analysis that selects appropriate text covering all phonetic units needed by the unit selection system. In addition to the statically defined sub-voices, the speech synthesis module implements dynamic transformations (e.g., emphasis), pauses, and variable speech speed. The system combines all these capabilities in order to dynamically modulate the synthesised speech to convey the impression of emotionally modulated speech.

3.5 Authoring

The interaction system is complemented by ELEON (Bilidas et al., 2007), an authoring tool for annotating domain ontologies with the generation and adaptivity resources described above. The domain ontology can be authored in ELEON, but any existing OWL ontology can also annotated.

More specifically, ELEON supports authoring *linguistic resources*, including a domain-dependent *lexicon*, which associates classes and individuals of the ontology with nouns and proper names of the target natural languages; *microplans*, which provide the NLG with patterns for realizing property instances as sentences; and a partial ordering of properties, which allows the system to order the resulting sentences as a coherent text.

The *adaptivity* and profiling resources include *interest rates*, indicating how interesting the entities of the ontology are in any given profile; and *stereotype parameters* that control generation aspects such as the number of facts to include in a description or the maximum sentence length.

Furthermore, ELEON supports the author with immediate previews, so that the effect of any change in either the ontology or the associated resources can be directly reviewed. The actual generation of the preview is relegated to external generation engines.

4 Conclusions

The demonstrated system combines semantic representation and reasoning technologies with language technology into a human-computer interaction system that exhibits a large degree of adaptability to audiences and circumstances and is able to take advantage of existing domain model created independently of the need to build a natural language interface. Furthermore by clearly separating the abstract, semantic layer from that of the linguistic realization, it allows the re-use of linguistic resources across domains and the domain model and adaptivity resources across languages.

Acknowledgements

The demonstrated system is being developed by the European (FP6-IST) project INDIGO.[3] INDIGO develops and advances human-robot interaction technology, enabling robots to perceive natural human behaviour, as well as making them act in ways that are more familiar to humans. To achieve its goals, INDIGO advances various technologies, which it integrates in a robotic platform.

References

Dimitris Bilidas, Maria Theologou, and Vangelis Karkaletsis. 2007. Enriching OWL ontologies with linguistic and user-related annotations: the ELEON system. In *Proc. 19th Intl. Conf. on Tools with Artificial Intelligence* (ICTAI-2007).

Robin Cooper and Staffan Larsson. 1998. Dialogue Moves and Information States. In: *Proceedings of the 3rd Intl. Workshop on Computational Semantics (IWCS-3).*

Stéphane Dupont. 2003. Robust parameters for noisy speech recognition. U.S. Patent 2003182114.

Dimitrios Galanis, George Karakatsiotis, Gerasimos Lampouras and Ion Androutsopoulos. 2009. An open-source natural language generator for OWL ontologies and its use in Protégé and Second Life. In this volume.

Stasinos Konstantopoulos, Vangelis Karkaletsis, and Colin Matheson. 2008. Robot personality: Representation and externalization. In *Proc. Computational Aspects of Affective and Emotional Interaction* (CAFFEi 08), Patras, Greece.

[3] http://www.ics.forth.gr/indigo/

Parsing, Projecting & Prototypes: Repurposing Linguistic Data on the Web

William D. Lewis
Microsoft Research
Redmond, WA 98052
wilewis@microsoft.com

Fei Xia
University of Washington
Seattle, WA 98195
fxia@u.washington.edu

1 Introduction

Until very recently, most NLP tasks (*e.g.*, parsing, tagging, etc.) have been confined to a very limited number of languages, the so-called majority languages. Now, as the field moves into the era of developing tools for Resource Poor Languages (RPLs)—a vast majority of the world's 7,000 languages are resource poor—the discipline is confronted not only with the algorithmic challenges of limited data, but also the sheer difficulty of locating data in the first place. In this demo, we present a resource which taps the large body of linguistically annotated data on the Web, data which can be repurposed for NLP tasks. Because the field of linguistics has as its mandate the study of human language—in fact, the study of *all* human language*s*—and has wholeheartedly embraced the Web as a means for disseminating linguistic knowledge, the consequence is that a large quantity of analyzed language data can be found on the Web. In many cases, the data is richly annotated and exists for many languages for which there would otherwise be very limited annotated data. The resource, the Online Database of INterlinear text (ODIN), makes this data available and provides additional annotation and structure, making the resource useful to the Computational Linguistic audience.

In this paper, after a brief discussion of the previous work on ODIN, we report our recent work on extending ODIN by applying machine learning methods to the task of data extraction and language identification, and on using ODIN to "discover" linguistic knowledge. Then we outline a plan for the demo presentation.

2 Background and Previous work on ODIN

ODIN is a collection of Interlinear Glossed Text (IGT) harvested from scholarly documents. In this section, we describe the original ODIN system (Lewis, 2006), and the IGT enrichment algorithm (Xia and Lewis, 2007). These serve as the starting point for our current work, which will be discussed in the next section.

2.1 Interlinear Glossed Text (IGT)

In recent years, a large part of linguistic scholarly discourse has migrated to the Web, whether it be in the form of papers informally posted to scholars' websites, or electronic editions of highly respected journals. Included in many papers are snippets of language data that are included as part of this linguistic discourse. The language data is often represented as Interlinear Glossed Text (IGT), an example of which is shown in (1).

(1) Rhoddodd yr athro lyfr i'r bachgen ddoe
gave-3sg the teacher book to-the boy yesterday
"The teacher gave a book to the boy yesterday"
(Bailyn, 2001)

The canonical form of an IGT consists of three lines: a *language line* for the language in question, a *gloss line* that contains a word-by-word or morpheme-by-morpheme gloss, and a *translation line*, usually in English. The grammatical annotations such as *3sg* on the gloss line are called *grams*.

2.2 The Original ODIN System

ODIN was built in three steps. First, linguistic documents that may contain instances of IGT are harvested from the Web using metacrawls. Metacrawling involves throwing queries against an existing search engine, such as Google and Live Search.

Second, IGT instances in the retrieved documents are identified using regular expression "templates", effectively looking for text that resembles IGT. An example RegEx template is shown in (2), which matches any three-line instance (e.g., the IGT instance in (1)) such that the first line starts with an example number (e.g., *(1)*) and the third line starts with a quotation mark.

(2)
```
\s*\(\d+\).*\n
\s*.*\n
\s*\['"].*\n
```

The third step is to determine the language of the language line in an IGT instance. Our original work in language ID relied on TextCat, an implementation of (Cavnar and Trenkle, 1994).

As of January 2008 (the time we started our current work), ODIN had 41,581 instances of IGT for 731 languages extracted from nearly 3,000 documents.[1]

[1]For a thorough discussion about how ODIN was originally constructed, see (Lewis, 2006).

Proceedings of the EACL 2009 Demonstrations Session, pages 41–44,
Athens, Greece, 3 April 2009.

2.3 Enriching IGT data

Since the language line in IGT data does not come with annotations (e.g., POS tags, phrase structures), Xia and Lewis (2007) proposed to enrich the original IGT and then extract syntactic information (e.g., context-free rules) to bootstrap NLP tools such as POS taggers and parsers. The enrichment algorithm has three steps: (1) parse the English translation with an English parser, (2) align the language line and the English translation via the gloss line, and (3) project syntactic structure from English to the language line. The algorithm was tested on 538 IGTs from seven languages and the word alignment accuracy was 94.1% and projection accuracy (i.e., the percentage of correct links in the projected dependency structures) was 81.5%.

3 Our recent work

We extend the previous work in three areas: (1) improving IGT detection and language identification, (2) testing the usefulness of the enriched IGT by answering typological questions, and (3) enhancing ODIN's search facility by allowing structural and "construction" searches.[2]

3.1 IGT detection

The canonical form of IGT, as presented in Section 2.1, consists of three parts and each part is on a single line. However, many IGT instances, 53.6% of instances in ODIN, do not follow the canonical format for various reasons. For instance, some IGT instances are missing gloss or translation lines as they can be recovered from context (*e.g.*, other neighboring examples or the text surrounding the instance); other IGT instances have multiple translations or language lines (e.g., one part in the native script, and another in a Latin transliteration).

Because of the irregular structure of IGT instances, the regular expression templates used in the original ODIN system performed poorly. We apply machine learning methods to the task. In particular, we treat the IGT detection task as a sequence labeling problem: we train a classifier to tag each line with a pre-defined tag set,[3] use the learner to tag new documents, and convert the best tag sequence into a span sequence. When trained on 41 documents (with 1573 IGT instances) and tested on 10 documents (with 447 instances), the F-score for *exact match* (i.e., two spans match iff they are identical) is 88.4%, and for *partial match* (i.e., two spans match iff they overlap) is 95.4%.[4] In comparison, the F-score of the RegEx approach on the same test set is 51.4% for exact match and 74.6% for partial match.

[2]By constructions, we mean linguistically salient constructions, such as actives, passives, relative clauses, inverted word orders, etc., in particular those we feel would be of the most benefit to linguists and computational linguists alike.

[3]The tagset extends the standard BIO tagging scheme.

[4]The result is produced by a Maximum Entropy learner. The results by SVM and CRF learners are similar. The details were reported in (Xia and Lewis, 2008).

Table 1: The language distribution of the IGTs in ODIN

Range of IGT instances	# of languages	# of IGT instances	% of IGT instances
> 10000	3	36,691	19.39
1000-9999	37	97,158	51.34
100-999	122	40,260	21.27
10-99	326	12,822	6.78
1-9	838	2,313	1.22
total	1326	189,244	100

3.2 Language ID

The language ID task here is very different from a typical language ID task. For instance, the number of languages in ODIN is more than a thousand and could potentially reach several thousand as more data is added. Furthermore, for most languages in ODIN, our training data contains few to no instances of IGT. Because of these properties, applying existing language ID algorithms to the task does not produce satisfactory results.

As IGTs are part of a document, there are often various cues in the document (e.g., language names) that can help predict the language ID of the IGT instances. We designed a new algorithm that treats the language ID task as a pronoun resolution task, where IGT instances are "pronouns", language names are "antecedents", and finding the language name of an IGT is the same as linking a pronoun (i.e., the IGT) to its antecedent (i.e., the language name). The algorithm outperforms existing, general-purpose language identification algorithms significantly. The detail of the algorithm and experimental results is described in (Xia et al., 2009).

Running the new IGT detection on the original three thousand ODIN documents, the number of IGT instances increases from 41,581 to 189,244. We then ran the new language ID algorithm on the IGTs, and Table 1 shows the language distribution of the IGTs in ODIN according to the output of the algorithm. For instance, the third row says that 122 languages each have 100 to 999 IGT instances, and the 40,260 instances in this bin account for 21.27% of all instances in ODIN.[5]

3.3 Answering typological questions

Linguistic typology is the study of the classification of languages, where a typology is an organization of languages by an enumerated list of logically possible types, most often identified by one or more structural features. One of the most well known and well studied typological types, or *parameters*, is that of canonical word order, made famous by Joseph Greenberg (Greenberg, 1963).

[5]Some IGTs are marked by the authors of the crawled documents as ungrammatical (usually with an asterisk "*" at the beginning of the language line). Those IGTs are kept in ODIN too because they could be useful to other linguists, the same reason that they were included in the original documents.

In (Lewis and Xia, 2008), we described a means for automatically discovering the answers to a number of computationally salient typological questions, such as the canonical order of constituents (e.g., sentential word order, order of constituents in noun phrases) or the existence of particular constituents in a language (e.g., definite or indefinite determiners). In these experiments, we tested not only the potential of IGT to provide knowledge that could be useful to NLP, but also for IGT to overcome biases inherent to the opportunistic nature of its collection: (1) What we call the *IGT-bias*, that is, the bias produced by the fact that IGT examples are used by authors to demonstrate a particular fact about a language, causing the collection of IGT for a language to suffer from a potential lack of representativeness. (2) What we call the *English-bias*, an English-centrism in the examples brought on by the fact that most IGT examples provide a translation in English, which can potentially affect subsequent enrichment of IGT data, such as through structural projection. In one experiment, we automatically found the answer to the canonical word order question for about 100 languages, and the accuracy was 99% for all the languages with at least 40 IGT instances.[6] In another experiment, our system answered 13 typological questions for 10 languages with an accuracy of 90%. The discovered knowledge can then be used for subsequent grammar and tool development work.

The knowledge we capture in IGT instances—both the native annotations provided by the linguists themselves, as well as the answers to a variety of typological questions discovered in IGT—we use to populate *language profiles*. These profiles are a recent addition to the ODIN site, and are available for those languages where sufficient data exists. Following is an example profile:

```
<Profile>
  <language code="WBP">Warlpiri</language>
  <ontologyNamespace prefix="gold">
     http://linguistic-ontology.org/gold.owl#
  </ontologyNamespace>
  <feature="word_order"><value>SVO</value></feature>
  <feature="det_order"><value>DT-NN</value></feature>
  <feature="case">
     <value>gold:DativeCase</value>
     <value>gold:ErgativeCase</value>
     <value>gold:NominativeCase</value>
                    . . .
</Profile>
```

3.4 Enhancing ODIN's Value to Computational Linguistics: Search and Language Profiles

ODIN provides a variety of ways to search across its data, in particular, search by language name or code, language family, and even by annotations and their related concepts. Once data is discovered that fits the particular pattern that a user is interested in, he/she can either display the data (where sufficient citation information exists and where the data is relatively clean) or locate documents in which the data exists. Additional search facilities allow users to search across potentially linguistically salient structures and return results in the form of language profiles. Although language profiles are by no means complete—they are subject to the availability of data to fill in the answers within the profiles—they provide a summary of automatically available knowledge about that language as found in IGT (or enriched IGT).

4 The Demo Presentation

Our focus in this demonstration will be on the query features of ODIN. In addition, however, we will also give some background on how ODIN was built, show how we see the data in ODIN being used by both the linguistic and NLP communities, and present the kind of information available in language profiles. The following is our plan for the demo:

- Very brief discussion on the methods used to build ODIN (as discussed in Section 2.2, 3.1, and 3.2)
- An overview of the IGT enrichment algorithm (as discussed in Section 2.3).
- A presentation of ODIN's search facility and the results that can be returned, in particular language profiles (as discussed in Section 3.3-3.4). ODIN's current website is **http://uakari.ling.washington.edu/odin**. Users can also search ODIN using the OLAC[7] search interfaces at the LDC[8] and LinguistList.[9] Some search examples are given below.

4.1 Example 1: Search by Language Name

The opening screen for ODIN allows the user to search the ODIN database by clicking a specific language name in the left-hand frame, or by typing all or part of a name (finding closest matches). Once a language is selected, our search tool will list all the documents that have data for the language in question. The user can then click on any of those documents, and search tool will return the IGT instances found in those documents. Following linguistic custom and fair use restrictions, only instances of data that have citations are displayed. An example is shown in Figure 1. Search by language and name is by far the most popular search in ODIN, given the hundreds of queries executed per day.

4.2 Example 2: Search by Linguistic Constructions

This type of query looks either at enriched data in the English translation, or at the projected structures in the

[6]Some IGT instances are not sentences and therefore are not useful for answering this question. Further, those instances marked as ungrammatical (usually with an asterisk "*") are ignored for this and all the typological questions.

[7]Open Language Archives Community

[8]http://www.language-archives.org/tools/search/

[9]LinguistList has graciously offered to host ODIN, and it is being migrated to http://odin.linguistlist.org. Completion of this migration is expected sometime in April 2009.

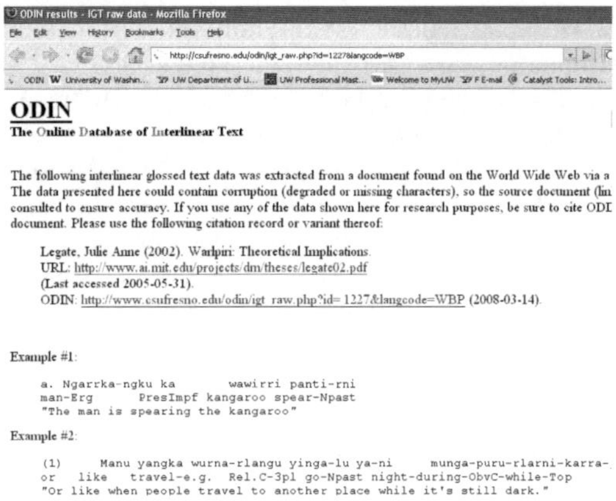

Figure 1: IGT instances in a document

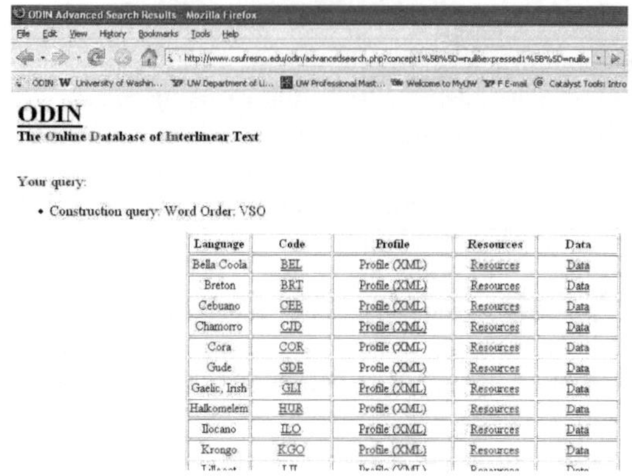

Figure 3: Languages in ODIN Determined to be VSO

target language data. Figure 2 shows the list of linguistic constructions that are currently covered.

Suppose the user clicks on "*Word Order: VSO*", the search tool will retrieve all the languages in ODIN that have VSO order according to the PCFGs extracted from the projected phrase structures (Figure 3). The user can then click on the *Data* link for any language in the list to retrieve the IGT instances in that language.

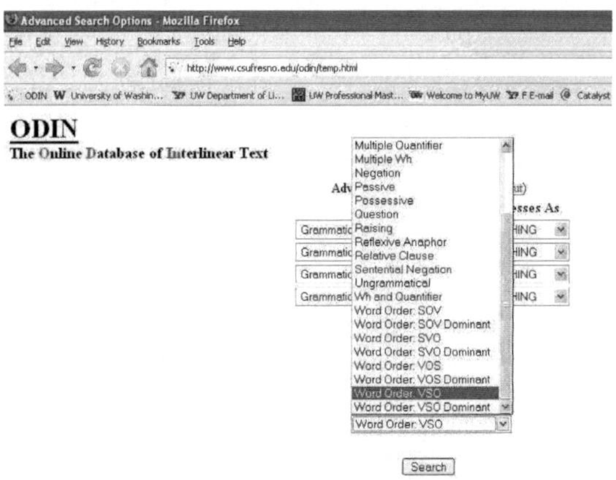

Figure 2: List of linguistic constructions that are currently supported

5 Conclusion

In this paper, we briefly discussed our work on improving the ODIN system, testing the usefulness of the ODIN data for linguistic study, and enhancing the search facility. While IGT data collected off the Web is inherently noisy, we show that even a sample size of 40 IGT instances is large enough to ensure 99% accuracy in predicting Word Order. In the future, we plan to continue our efforts to collect more data for ODIN, in order to make it a more useful resource to the linguistic and computational linguistic audiences. Likewise, we will further extend the search interface to allow more sophisticated queries that tap the full breadth of languages that exist in ODIN, and give users greater access to the enriched annotations and projected structures that can be found only in ODIN.

References

John Frederick Bailyn. 2001. Inversion, Dislocation and Optionality in Russian. In Gerhild Zybatow, editor, *Current Issues in Formal Slavic Linguistics*.

W. B. Cavnar and J. M. Trenkle. 1994. N-gram-based text categorization. In *Proceedings of Third Annual Symposium on Document Analysis and Information Retrieval*, pages 161–175, Las Vegas, April.

Joseph H. Greenberg. 1963. Some universals of grammar with particular reference to the order of meaningful elements. In Joseph H. Greenberg, editor, *Universals of Language*, pages 73–113. MIT Press, Cambridge, Massachusetts.

William D. Lewis and Fei Xia. 2008. Automatically Identifying Computationally Relevant Typological Features. In *Proceedings of The Third International Joint Conference on Natural Language Processing (IJCNLP)*, Hyderabad, January.

William D. Lewis. 2006. ODIN: A Model for Adapting and Enriching Legacy Infrastructure. In *Proceedings of the e-Humanities Workshop*, Amsterdam. Held in cooperation with e-Science 2006: 2nd IEEE International Conference on e-Science and Grid Computing.

Fei Xia and William D. Lewis. 2007. Multilingual structural projection across interlinearized text. In *Proceedings of the North American Association of Computational Linguistics (NAACL) conference*.

Fei Xia and William D. Lewis. 2008. Repurposing Theoretical Linguistic Data for Tool Development and Search. In *Proceedings of The Third International Joint Conference on Natural Language Processing (IJCNLP)*, Hyderabad, January.

Fei Xia, William D. Lewis, and Hoifung Poon. 2009. Language ID in the Context of Harvesting Language Data off the Web. In *Proceedings of The 12th Conference of the European Chapter of the Association of Computational Linguistics (EACL)*, Athens, Greece, April.

A Tool for Multi-Word Expression Extraction in Modern Greek Using Syntactic Parsing

Athina Michou
University of Geneva
Geneva, Switzerland
Athina.Michou@unige.ch

Violeta Seretan
University of Geneva
Geneva, Switzerland
Violeta.Seretan@unige.ch

Abstract

This paper presents a tool for extracting multi-word expressions from corpora in Modern Greek, which is used together with a parallel concordancer to augment the lexicon of a rule-based machine-translation system. The tool is part of a larger extraction system that relies, in turn, on a multilingual parser developed over the past decade in our laboratory. The paper reviews the various NLP modules and resources which enable the retrieval of Greek multi-word expressions and their translations: the Greek parser, its lexical database, the extraction and concordancing system.

1 Introduction

In today's multilingual society, there is a pressing need for building translation resources, such as large-coverage multilingual lexicons, translation systems or translation aid tools, especially due to the increasing interest in computer-assisted translation.

This paper presents a tool intended to assist translators/lexicographers dealing with Greek[1] as a source or a target language. The tool deals specifically with multi-lexeme lexical items, also called *multi-word expressions* (henceforth MWEs). Its main functionalities are: 1) the robust parsing of Greek text corpora and the syntax-based detection of word combinations that are likely to constitute MWEs, and 2) concordance and alignment functions supporting the manual creation of monolingual and bilingual MWE lexicons.

The tool relies on a symbolic parsing technology, and is part of FipsCo, a larger extraction system (Seretan, 2008) which has previously been used to build MWE resources for other languages, including English, French, Spanish, and Italian. Its extension to Greek will ultimately enable the inclusion of this language in the list of languages supported by an in-house translation system.

The paper is structured as follows. Section 2 introduces the Greek parser and its lexical database. Section 3 provides a description of Greek MWEs, including a syntactic classification for these. Section 4 presents the extraction tool, and Section 5 concludes the paper.

2 The Greek parser

The Greek parser is part of Fips, a multilingual symbolic parser that deals, among other languages, with English, French, Spanish, Italian, and German (Wehrli, 2007). The Greek version, FipsGreek (Michou, 2007), has recently reached an acceptable level of lexical and grammatical coverage.

Fips relies on generative grammar concepts, and is basically made up of a generic parsing module which can be refined in order to suit the specific needs of a particular language. Currently, there are approximately 60 grammar rules defined for Greek, allowing for the complete parse of about 50% of the sentences in a corpus like Europarl (Koehn, 2005), which contains proceedings of the European Parliament. For the remaining sentences, partial analyses are instead proposed for the chunks identified.

One of the key components of the parser is its (manually-built) lexicon. It contains detailed morphosyntactic and semantic information, namely, selectional properties, subcategorization information, and syntactico-semantic features that are likely to influence the syntactic analysis.

The Greek monolingual lexicon presently contains about 110000 words corresponding to 16000

[1] For the sake of simplicity, we will henceforth use the term Greek to refer to Modern Greek.

Proceedings of the EACL 2009 Demonstrations Session, pages 45–48,
Athens, Greece, 3 April 2009. ©2009 Association for Computational Linguistics

lexemes,[2] and a limited number of MWEs (about 500). The bilingual lexicon used by our translation system contains slightly more than 8000 Greek-French/French-Greek equivalents.

3 MWEs in Modern Greek

Greek is a language which exhibits a high MWE productivity, with new compound words being created especially in the science and technology domains. Sometimes, existing words are transformed in order to denote new concepts; also, numerous neologisms are created or borrowed from other languages.

A frequent type of multi-word constructions in Greek are special noun phrases, called *lexical phrases* (Anastasiadi-Symeonidi, 1986) or *loose multi-word compounds* (Ralli, 2005):

- Adjective+Noun: ανοιχτή θάλασσα (`anichti thalassa`, 'open sea'), παιδική χαρά (`pediki chara`, 'kindergarten');
- Noun+Noun$_{GEN}$: ζώνη ασφαλείας (`zoni asfalias`, 'safety belt'), φόρος εισοδήματος (`foros isodimatos`, 'income tax');
- Noun+Noun$_{NOM}$ (head-complement relation): παιδί-θαύμα (`pedi-thavma`, 'child prodigy'), συζήτηση-μαραθώνιος (`syzitisi-marathonios`, 'marathon talks') ;
- Noun$_{NOM}$+Noun$_{NOM}$ (coordination relation): καναπές-κρεβάτι (`kanapes-krevati`, 'sofa bed'), γιατρός-νοσοκόμος (`yiatros-nosokomos`, 'doctor-nurse').

A large body of Greek MWEs constitute *collocations* (typical word associations whose meaning is easy to decode, but whose component items are difficult to predict), such as καταρρίπτω ένα ρεκόρ (`kataripto ena rekor`, 'to break a record'), in which the verbal collocate καταρρίπτω ('shake down') is unpredictable. Collocations may occur in a wide range of syntactic types. Some of the configurations taken into account in our work are:

- Noun(Subject)+Verb: η συζήτηση λήγει (`i sizitisi liyi`, 'discussion ends');
- Adjective+Noun: θανατική ποινή (`thanatiki pini`, 'death penalty');
- Verb+Noun(Object): διατρέχω κίνδυνο (`diatrecho kindino`, 'run a risk');
- Verb+Preposition+Noun(Argument): καταδικάζω σε θάνατο (`katadikazo se thanato`, 'to sentence to death');
- Verb+Preposition: προσανατολίζομαι προς (`prosanatolizome pros`, 'to orient to');
- Noun+Preposition+Noun: προτροπή για ανάπτυξη (`protropi yia anaptiksi`, 'incitement to development');
- Preposition+Noun: υπό συζήτηση (`ipo sizitisi`, 'under discussion');
- Verb+Adverb: χειροκροτώ θερμά (`xirokroto therma`, 'applause warmly');
- Adverb+Adjective: γενετικά τροποποιημένος (`yenetika tropopiimenos`, 'genetically modified');
- Adjective+Preposition: εξαρτημένος από (`eksartimenos apo`, 'dependent on').

In addition, Greek MWEs cover other types of constructions, such as:

- one-word compounds: ερυθρόδερμος (`erithrodermos`, 'red skin'), λυκόσκυλο (`likoskylo`, 'wolfhound');
- adverbial phrases: εκ των προτέρων (`ek ton proteron`, 'a priori, in principle');
- idiomatic expressions (whose meaning is difficult to decode): γίνομαι χαλί να με πατήσεις (`yinome xali na me patisis`, literally, *become a carpet to walk all over*; 'be ready to satisfy any wish').

4 The MWE Extraction Tool

MWEs constitute a high proportion of the lexicon of a language, and are crucial for many NLP tasks (Sag et al., 2002). This section introduces the tool we developed for augmenting the coverage of our monolingual/bilingual MWE lexicons.

4.1 Extraction

As we already mentioned, the Greek MWE extractor is part of FipsCo, a larger extraction system based on a symbolic parsing technology (Seretan, 2008) which we previously applied on text corpora in other languages. The recent development of the Greek parser enabled us to extend it and apply it to Greek.

[2] Most of the inflected forms were automatically obtained through morphological generation; that is, the base word was combined with the appropriate suffixes, according to a given inflectional paradigm. A number of 25 inflection classes have been defined for Greek nouns, 11 for verbs, and 10 for adjectives.

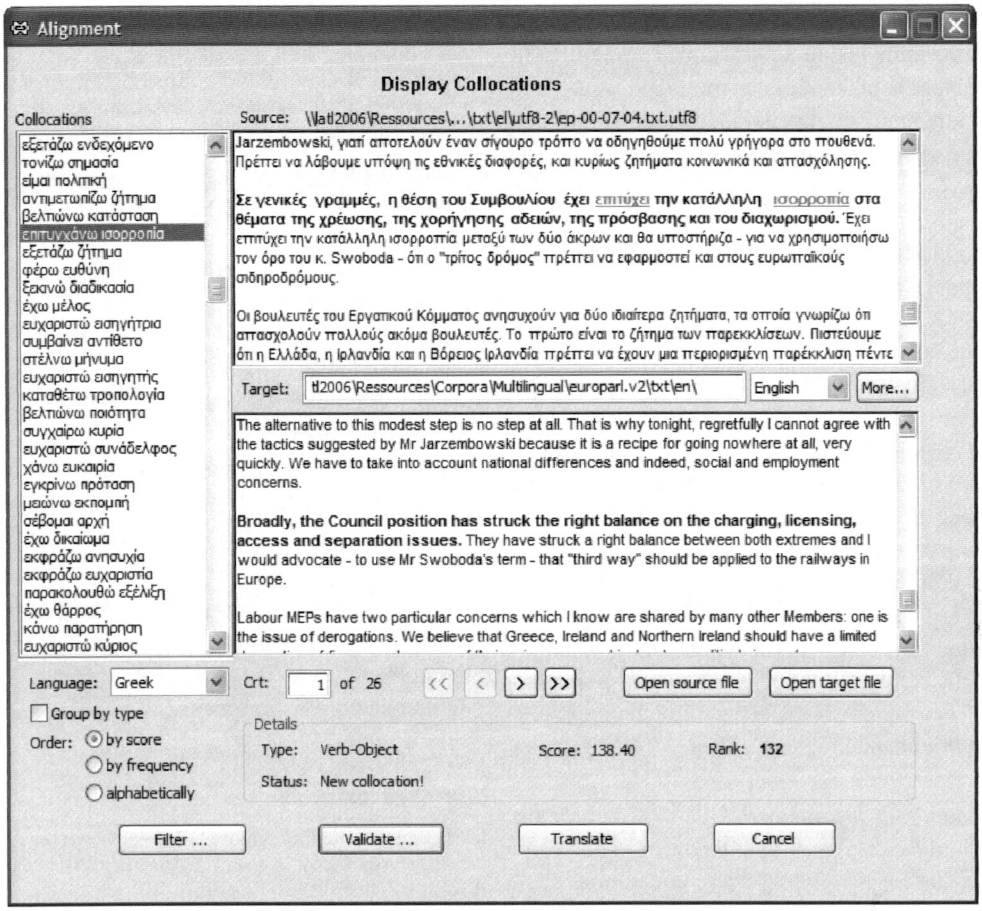

Figure 1: Screen capture of the parallel concordancer, showing an instance of the collocation επιτυγχάνω ισορροπία ('strike balance') and the aligned context in the target language, English.

The extractor is designed as a module which is plugged into the parser. After a sentence from the source corpus is parsed, the extractor traverses the output structure and identifies as a potential MWE the words found in one of the syntactic configurations listed in Section 3.

Once all MWE candidates are collected from the corpus, they are divided into subsets according to their syntactic configuration. Then, each subset undergo a statistical analysis process whose aim is to detect those candidates that are highly cohesive. A strong association between the items of a candidate indicates that this is likely to constitute a collocation. The strength of association can be measured with one of the numerous association measures implemented in our extractor. By default, the log-likelihood ratio measure (LLR) is proposed, since it was shown to be particularly suited to language data (Dunning, 1993).

In our extractor, the items of each candidate expression represent base word forms (lemmas) and they are considered in the canonical order implied by the given syntactic configuration (e.g., for a verb-object candidate, the object is postverbal in SVO languages like Greek). Even if the candidate occurs in corpus in a different morphosyntactic realizations, its various occurrences are successfully identified as instances of the same type thanks to the syntactic analysis performed with the parser.

4.2 Visualization

The extraction tool also provides visualization functions which facilitate the consultation and interpretation of results by users—e.g., lexicographers, terminologists, translators, language learners—by displaying them in the original context. The following functions are provided:

Filtering and sorting The results which will be displayed can be selected according to several criteria: the syntactic configuration (i.e., users can select only one or several configurations they are interested in), the LLR score, the corpus frequency (users can specify the limits of the desired interval),[3] the words involved (users can look up MWEs containing specific words). Also, the selected results can be ordered by score or frequency, and users can filter them according to the rank obtained.

Concordance The (filtered) results are displayed on a concordancing interface, similar to the one shown in Figure 1. The list on the left shows the MWE candidates that were extracted. When an item of the list is selected, the text panel on the right displays the context of its first instance in the source document. The arrow buttons beneath allow users to navigate through all the instances of that candidate. The whole content of the source document is accessible, and it is automatically scrolled to the current instance; the component words and the sentence in which they occur are highlighted in different colors.

Alignment If parallel corpora are available, the results can be displayed in a sentence-aligned context. That is, the equivalent of the source sentence in the target document containing the translation of the source document is also automatically found, highlighted and displayed next to the original context (see Figure 1). Thus, users can see how a MWE has previously been translated in a given context.

Validation The tool also provides functionalities allowing users to create a database of manually validated MWEs from among the candidates displayed on the (parallel) concordancing interfaces. The database can store either monolingual or bilingual entries; most of the information associated to an entry—such as lexeme indexes, syntactic type, source sentence—is automatically filled-in by the system. For bilingual entries, a translation must be provided by the user, and this can be easily retrieved manually from the target sentence showed in the parallel concordancer (thus, for the collocation shown in Figure 1, the user can find the English equivalent *strike balance*).

[3]Thus, users can specify themselves a threshold (in other systems it is arbitrarily predefined).

5 Conclusion

We presented a MWE extractor with advanced concordancing functions, which can be used to semi-automatically build Greek monolingual/bilingual MWE lexicons. It relies on a deep syntactic approach, whose benefits are manifold: retrieval of grammatical results, interpretation of syntactic constituents in terms of arguments, disambiguation of lexemes with multiple readings, and grouping of all morphosyntactic variants of MWEs.

Our system is most similar to Termight (Dagan and Church, 1994) and TransSearch (Macklovitch et al., 2000). To our knowledge, it is the first of this type for Greek.

Acknowledgements

This work has been supported by the Swiss National Science Foundation (grant 100012-117944). The authors would like to thank Eric Wehrli for his support and useful comments.

References

Anna Anastasiadi-Symeonidi. 1986. *The neology in the Common Modern Greek*. Triandafyllidi's foundation, Thessaloniki. In Greek.

Ido Dagan and Kenneth Church. 1994. *Termight*: Identifying and translating technical terminology. In *Proceedings of ANLP*, pages 34–40, Stuttgart, Germany.

Ted Dunning. 1993. Accurate methods for the statistics of surprise and coincidence. *Computational Linguistics*, 19(1):61–74.

Philipp Koehn. 2005. Europarl: A parallel corpus for statistical machine translation. In *Proceedings of MT Summit X*, pages 79–86, Phuket, Thailand.

Elliott Macklovitch, Michel Simard, and Philippe Langlais. 2000. TransSearch: A free translation memory on the World Wide Web. In *Proceedings of LREC 2000*, pages 1201–1208, Athens, Greece.

Athina Michou. 2007. Analyse syntaxique et traitement automatique du syntagme nominal grec moderne. In *Proceedings of TALN 2007*, pages 203–212, Toulouse, France.

Angela Ralli. 2005. *Morphology*. Patakis, Athens. In Greek.

Ivan A. Sag, Timothy Baldwin, Francis Bond, Ann Copestake, and Dan Flickinger. 2002. Multiword expressions: A pain in the neck for NLP. In *Proceedings of CICLING 2002*, pages 1–15, Mexico City.

Violeta Seretan. 2008. *Collocation extraction based on syntactic parsing*. Ph.D. thesis, University of Geneva.

Eric Wehrli. 2007. Fips, a "deep" linguistic multilingual parser. In *Proceedings of ACL 2007 Workshop on Deep Linguistic Processing*, pages 120–127, Prague, Czech Republic.

Matching Readers' Preferences and Reading Skills with Appropriate Web Texts

Eleni Miltsakaki
University of Pennsylvania
Philadelphia, U.S.A.
elenimi@seas.upenn.edu

Abstract

This paper describes Read-X, a system designed to identify text that is *appropriate* for the reader given his thematic choices and the reading ability associated with his educational background. To our knowledge, Read-X is the first web-based system that performs real-time searches and returns results classified thematically and by reading level within seconds. To facilitate educators or students searching for reading material at specific reading levels, Read-X extracts the text from the html, pdf, doc, or xml format and makes available a text editor for viewing and editing the extracted text.

1 Introduction

The automatic analysis and categorization of web text has witnessed a booming interest due to increased text availability of different formats (txt, ppt, pdf, etc), content, genre and authorship. The web is witnessing an unprecedented explosion in text variability. Texts are contributed by users of varied reading and writing skills as opposed to the earlier days of the Internet when text was mostly published by companies or institutions. The age range of web users has also widened to include very young school and sometimes pre-school aged readers. In schools the use of the Internet is now common to many classes and homework assignments. However, while the *relevance* of web search results to given keywords has improved substantially over the past decade, the *appropriateness* of the results is uncatered for. On a keyword search for 'snakes' the same results will be given whether the user is a seven year old elementary school kid or a snake expert.

Prior work on assessing reading level includes (Heilman et al., 2007) who experiment with a system that employs grammatical features and vocabulary to predict readability. The system is part of the the REAP tutor, designed to help ESL learners improve their vocabulary skills. REAP's information retrieval system (Collins-Thompson and Callan, 2004) is based on web data that have been annotated and indexed off-line. Also, relatedly, (Schwarm and Ostendorf, 2005) use a statistical language model to train SVM classifiers to classify text for grade levels 2-5. The classifier's precision ranges from 38%- 75% depending on the grade level.

In this demo, we present Read-X, a system designed to evaluate if text retrieved from the web is appropriate for the intended reader. Our system analyzes web text and returns the thematic area and the expected reading difficulty of the retrieved texts. [1] To our knowledge, Read-X is the first system that performs *in real time* a)keyword search, b)thematic classification and c)analysis of reading difficulty. Search results and analyses are returned within a few seconds to a maximum of a minute or two depending on the speed of the connection. Read-X is enhanced with an added component which predicts difficult vocabulary given the user's educational level and familiarity with specific thematic areas.

2 Web search and text classification

Internet search. Read-X uses Yahoo! Web Services to execute the keyword search. When the search button is clicked or the enter key depressed after typing in a keyword, Read-X sends a search request to Yahoo! including the keywords and, optionally, the number of results to return.

Text extraction. The html, xml, doc or pdf documents stored at each URL are then extracted in a cleaned-up, tag-free, text format. At this stage a decision is made as to whether a web page contains reading material and not "junk". This is a non-trivial task. (Petersen and Ostendorf, 2006) use a classifier for this task with moderate success. We "read" the structure of the html text to decide if the content is appropriate and when in doubt, we

[1] A demo video can be accessed at the blogsite www.eacl08demo.blogspot.com.

Proceedings of the EACL 2009 Demonstrations Session, pages 49–52,
Athens, Greece, 3 April 2009. ©2009 Association for Computational Linguistics

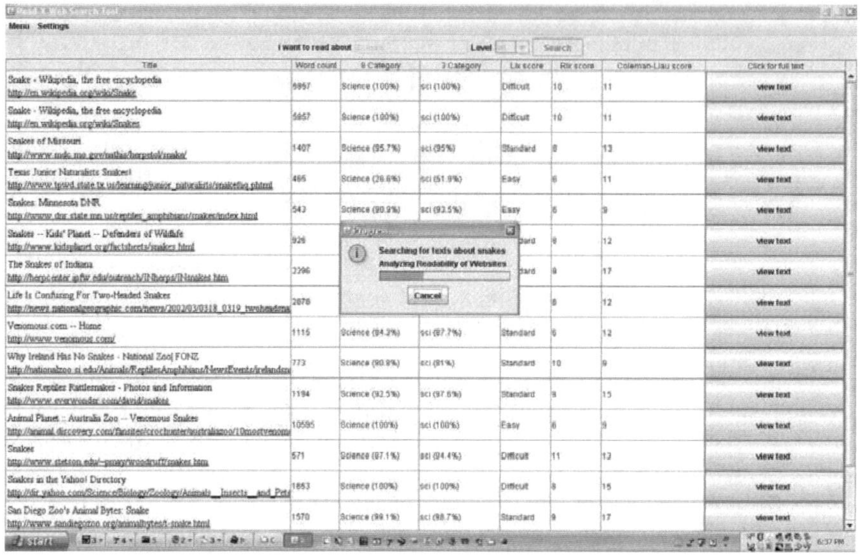

Figure 1: Search results and analysis of readability

err on the side of throwing out potentially useful content.

Readability analysis. For printed materials, there are a number of readability formulas used to measure the difficulty of a given text; the New Dale-Chall Readability Formula, The Fry Readability Formula, the Gunning-Fog Index, the Automated Readability Index, and the Flesch Kincaid Reading Ease Formula are a few examples (see (DuBay, 2007) for an overview and references). Usually, these formulas count the number of syllables, long sentences, or difficult words in randomly selected passages of the text. To automate the process of readability analysis, we chose three Readability algorithms: Lix, RIX, see (Anderson, 1983), and Coleman-Liau, (Coleman and Liau, 1975), which were best suited for fast calculation and provide the user with either an approximate grade level for the text or a readability classification of very easy, easy, standard, difficult or very difficult. When each text is analyzed, the following statistics are computed: total number of sentences, total number of words, total number of long words (seven or more characters), and total number of letters in the text. Steps have been taken to develop more sophisticated measures for future implementations. Our current research aims at implementing more sophisticated reading difficulty measures, including reader's familiarity with the topic, metrics of propositional density and discourse coherence, without compromising speed of processing.

Formula	**r3**	**r4**	**r5**
Lix	10.2 (9-11)	11.7 (10-13)	11.1 (9-12)
RIX	10.2 (8-13)	12.3 (10-13)	11.5 (10-13)
Coleman-Liau	11.65 (9.2-13.3)	12.67 (12.2-13.1)	12.6 (11.4-14.1)
All	10.6	12.3	11.7

Table 1: Comparison of scores from three readability formulae.

To evaluate the performance of the reading scores we used as groundtruth a corpus of web-texts classified for readability levels r3, r4, r5 corresponding to grade levels 7-8, 9-10, and 11-13 respectively.[2] The content of the corpus is a collection of web-sites with educational content, picked by secondary education teachers. For 90 documents, randomly selected from levels 3-5 (30 per level), we computed the scores predicted by Lix, RIX and Coleman-Liau.

The average scores assigned by the three formulas are shown in Table (1). The numbers in parentheses show the range of scores assigned by each formula for the collection of documents under each reading level. The average score of all formulas for r3 is 10.6 which is sufficiently differentiated from the average 12.3. for r4. The average score of all formulas for r5, however, is 11.7, which cannot be used to differentiate r4 from r5. These results indicate that at least by comparison to the data in

[2]With the exception of Spache and Powers-Sumner-Kearl test, all other readability formulas are not designed for low grade readability levels.

Classifier	Basic categories	Subcategories
Naive Bayes	66%	30%
MaxEnt	78%	66%
MIRA	76%	58%

Table 2: Performance of text classifiers.

our corpus, the formulas can make reasonable distinctions between middle school and high school grades but they cannot make finer distinctions between different high-school grades. A more reliable form of evaluation is currently underway. We have designed self-paced reading experiments for different readability scores produced by five formulas (RIX, Lix, Coleman-Liau, Flesch-Kincaid and Dale-Chall). Formulas whose predictions will more closely reflect reading times for text comprehension will be preferred and form the basis for a better metric in the future. In the current implementation, Read-X reports the scores for each formula in a separate column. Other readability features modeling aspects of discourse coherence (e.g.,(Miltsakaki and Kukich, 2004), (Barzilay and Lapata, 2008), (Bruss et al., 2004), (Pitler and Nenkova, 2008)) can also be integrated after psycholinguistic evaluation studies are completed and their computation of such features can be made in real time.

Text classification For the text classification task, we a) built a corpus of prelabeled thematic categories and b) compared the performance of three classifiers to evaluate their suitability for thematic classification task.[3]

We collected a corpus of approximately 3.4 million words. The corpus contains text extracted from web-pages that were previously manually classified per school subject area by educators. We organized it into a small thematic hierarchy, with three sets of labels: a) labels for supercategories, b) labels for basic categories and c) labels for subcategories. There are 3 supercategories (Literature, Science, Sports), 8 basic categories (Arts, Career and Business, Literature, Philosophy and Religion, Science, Social studies, Sports and health, Technology) and 41 subcategories (e.g., the subcategories for Literature are Art Criticism, Art History, Dance, Music, Theater).

The performance of the classifiers trained on the basic categories and subcategories data is shown in Table (2). All classifiers perform reasonably well in the basic categories classification task but are outperformed by the MaxEnt classifier in both the basic categories and subcategories classifications. The supercategories classification by MaxEnt (not shown in the Table) is 93%. As expected, the performance of the classifiers deteriorates substantially for the subcategories task. This is expected due to the large number of labels and the small size of data available for each subcategory. We expect that as we collect more data the performance of the classifiers for this task will improve.

In the demo version, Read-X uses only the MaxEnt classifier to assign thematic labels and reports results for the super categories and basic categories, which have been tested and shown to be reliable.

3 Predicting difficult words given reader's background

The analysis of reading difficulty based on standard readability formulas gives a quick and easy way to measure reading difficulty but these formulas lack sophistication and sensitivity to the abilities and background of readers. They are reasonably good at making rough distinctions between -standardly defined- middle, high-school or college levels but they fall short in predicting reading ease or difficulty for specific readers. For example, a reader who is familiar with literary texts will have less difficulty reading new literary text than a reader, with a similar educational background, who has never read any literary works. In this section, we discuss the first step we have taken towards making more reliable evaluations of text readability given the profile of the reader.

Readers who are familiar with specific thematic areas, are more likely to know vocabulary that is recurring in these areas. So, if we have vocabulary frequency counts per thematic area, we are in a better position to predict difficult words for specific readers given their reading profiles. Vocabulary frequency lists are often used by test developers as an indicator of text difficulty, based on the assumption that less frequent words are more likely to be unknown. However, these lists are built from a variety of themes and cannot be customized for the reader. We have computed vocabulary frequencies for all the basic thematic categories in our corpus. The top 10 most frequent words per supercategory are shown in Table (3).

[3]We gratefully acknowledge MALLET, a collection of statistical NLP tools written in Java, publicly available at `http://mallet.cs.umass.edu` and Mark Dredze for his help installing and running MIRA on our data.

Arts	Career and Business	Literature	Philosophy	Science	Social Studies	Sports, Health	Technology
Word Freq	Word Freq	Word Freq	Word Freq t	Word Freq	Word Freq	Word Freq	Word Freq
musical 166	product 257	seemed 1398	argument 174	trees 831	behavior 258	players 508	software 584
leonardo 166	income 205	myself 1257	knowledge 158	bacteria 641	states 247	league 443	computer 432
instrument 155	market 194	friend 1255	augustine 148	used 560	psychoanalytic 222	player 435	site 333
horn 149	price 182	looked 1231	belief 141	growth 486	social 198	soccer 396	video 308
banjo 128	cash 178	things 1153	memory 130	acid 476	clemency 167	football 359	games 303
american 122	analysis 171	caesar 1059	truth 130	years 472	psychology 157	games 320	used 220
used 119	resources 165	going 1051	logic 129	alfalfa 386	psychotherapy 147	teams 292	systems 200
nature 111	positioning 164	having 1050	things 125	crop 368	united 132	national 273	programming 174
artist 104	used 153	asked 1023	existence 115	species 341	society 131	years 263	using 172
wright 98	sales 151	indeed 995	informal 113	acre 332	court 113	season 224	engineering 170

Table 3: 10 top most frequent words per thematic category.

Vocabulary frequencies per grade level have also been computed but they are not shown here.

We have added a special component to the Read-X architecture, which is designed to predict unknown vocabulary given the reader's educational background or familiarity with one (or more) of the basic themes. The interface allows you to select a web search result for further analysis. The user can customize vocabulary difficulty predictions by selecting the desired grade or theme. Then, the text is analyzed and, in a few seconds, it returns the results of the analysis. The vocabulary evaluator checks the vocabulary frequency of the words in the text and highlights the words that do not rank high in the vocabulary frequency index for the chosen categories (grade or theme). The highlighted words are clickable. When they are clicked, the entry information from WordNet appears on the right panel. The system has not been evaluated yet so some tuning will be required to determine the optimal cut-off frequency point for highlighting words.

4 Future work

A major obstacle in developing better readability models is the lack of reliable 'groundtruth' data. Annotated data are very scarce but even such data are only partially useful as it is not known if inter-annotator agreement for readability levels would be high. To address this issue we are currently running a battery of self-paced reading and eye-tracking experiments a) to evaluate which, if any, readability formulas accurately predict differences in reading times b)to test new hypotheses about possible factors affecting the perceived difficulty of a text, including vocabulary familiarity, propositional density and discourse coherence.

Acknowledgments

Audrey Troutt developed the software for Read-X under a GAPSA Provost's Award for Interdisciplinary Innovation, University of Pennsylvania.

References

Jonathan Anderson. 1983. Lix and rix: Variations of a little-known readability index. *Journal of Reading*, 26(6):490–496.

Regina Barzilay and Mirella Lapata. 2008. Modeling local coherence: An entity-based approach. *Computational Linguistics*.

M. Bruss, M. J. Albers, and D. S. McNamara. 2004. Changes in scientific articles over two hundred years: A coh-metrix analysis. In *Proceedings of the 22nd Annual International Conference on Design of Communication: the Engineering of Quality Documentation*, pages 104–109. New York: ACM Press.

M Coleman and T. Liau. 1975. A computer readability formula designed for machine scoring. *Journal of Applied Psychology*, 60:283–284.

K. Collins-Thompson and J. Callan. 2004. Information retrieval for language tutoring: An overview of the REAP project. In *Proceedings of the Twenty Seventh Annual International ACM SIGIR Conference on Research and Development in Information Retrieval (poster descritpion.*

William DuBay. 2007. *Smart Language: Readers, Readability, and the Grading of Text.* BookSurge Publishing. overview of readability formulas and references.

M. Heilman, K. Collins-Thompson, J. Callan, and M. Eskenazi. 2007. Combining lexical and grammatical features to improve readability measures for first and second language texts. In *Proceedings of the Human Language Technology Conference. Rochester, NY.*

Eleni Miltsakaki and Karen Kukich. 2004. Evaluation of text coherence for electronic essay scoring systems. *Natural Language Engineering*, 10(1).

Sarah Petersen and Mari Ostendorf. 2006. Assessing the reading level of web pages. In *Proceedings of Interspeech 2006 (poster)*, pages 833–836.

Emily Pitler and Ani Nenkova. 2008. Revisiting readability: A unified framework for predicting text quality. In *Proceedings of EMNLP, 2008.*

Sarah E. Schwarm and Mari Ostendorf. 2005. Reading level assessment using support vector machines and statistical language models. In *ACL '05: Proceedings of the 43rd Annual Meeting on Association for Computational Linguistics*, pages 523–530.

A text-based search interface for Multimedia Dialectics

Katerina Pastra
Inst. for Language & Speech Processing
Athens, Greece
kpastra@ilsp.gr

Eirini Balta
Inst. for Language & Speech Processing
Athens, Greece
ebalta@ilsp.gr

Abstract

The growing popularity of multimedia documents requires language technologies to approach automatic language analysis and generation from yet another perspective: that of its use in multimodal communication. In this paper, we present a support tool for COSMOROE, a theoretical framework for modelling multimedia dialectics. The tool is a text-based search interface that facilitates the exploration of a corpus of audiovisual files, annotated with the COSMOROE relations.

1 Introduction

Online multimedia content becomes more and more accessible through digital TV, social networking sites and searchable digital libraries of photographs and videos. People of different ages and cultures attempt to make sense out of this data and re-package it for their own needs, these being informative, educational and entertainment ones. Understanding and generation of multimedia discourse requires knowledge and skills related to the *nature* of the interacting modalities and their *semantic interplay* for formulating the multimedia message.

Within such context, intelligent multimedia systems are expected to parse/generate such messages or at least assist humans in these tasks. From another perspective, everyday human communication is predominantly multimodal; as such, similarly intuitive human-computer/robot interaction demands that intelligent systems master —among others— the semantic interplay between different media and modalities, i.e. they are able to use/understand natural language and its reference to objects and activities in the shared, situated communication space.

It was more than a decade ago, when the lack of a theory of how different media interact with one another was indicated (Whittaker and Walker, 1991). Recently, such theoretical framework has been developed and used for annotating a corpus of audiovisual documents with the objective of using such corpus for developing multimedia information processing tools (Pastra, 2008). In this paper, we provide a brief overview of the theory and the corresponding annotated corpus and present a text-based search interface that has been developed for the exploration and the automatic expansion/generalisation of the annotated semantic relations. This search interface is a support tool for the theory and the related corpus and a first step towards its computational exploitation.

2 COSMOROE

The CrOSs-Media inteRactiOn rElations (COSMOROE) framework describes multimedia dialectics, i.e. the semantic interplay between images, language and body movements (Pastra, 2008). It uses an *analogy to language discourse* analysis for "talking" about multimedia dialectics. It actually borrows terms that are widely used in language analysis for describing a number of phenomena (e.g. metonymy, adjuncts etc.) and adopts a message-formation perspective which is reminiscent of *structuralistic* approaches in language description. While doing so, inherent characteristics of the different modalities (e.g. exhaustive specificity of images) are taken into consideration.

COSMOROE is the result of a *thorough, inter-disciplinary review* of image-language and gesture-language interaction relations and characteristics, as described across a number of disciplines from computational and semiotic perspectives. It is also the result of *observation and analysis* of different types of corpora for different tasks. COSMOROE was tested for its coverage and descriptive power through the annotation of a corpus of TV travel documentaries. Figure 1 presents the COSMOROE relations. There are three main rela-

Proceedings of the EACL 2009 Demonstrations Session, pages 53–56,
Athens, Greece, 3 April 2009.

tions: semantic equivalence, complementarity and independence, each with each own subtypes.

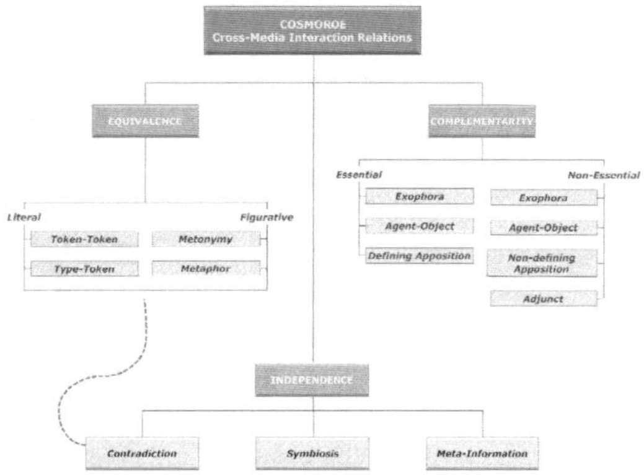

Figure 1: The COSMOROE cross-media relations

For annotating a corpus with the COSMOROE relations, a multi-faceted annotation scheme is employed. COSMOROE relations link two or more annotation facets, *i.e.* the modalities of two or more different media. Time offsets of the transcribed speech, subtitles, graphic-text and scene text, body movements, gestures, shots (with foreground and background distinction) and keyframe-regions are identified and included in COSMOROE relations. All visual data have been labelled by the annotators with one or two-word action or entity denoting tags. These labels have resulted from a process of watching only the visual stream of the file. The labelling followed a cognitive categorisation approach, that builds on the "basic level theory" of categorisation (Rosch, 1978). Currently, the annotated corpus consists of 5 hours of TV travel documentaries in Greek and 5 hours of TV travel documentaries in English. Three hours of the Greek files have undergone validation and a preliminary inter-annotator agreement study has also been carried out (Pastra, 2008).

3 The COSMOROE Search Interface

Such rich semantically annotated multimedia corpus requires a support tool that will serve the following:

- it will facilitate the active exploration and presentation of the semantic interplay between different modalities for any user, illustrating the COSMOROE theory through specific examples from real audiovisual data
- it will serve as simple search interface for general users, taking advantage of the rich semantic annotation —behind the scenes— for more precise and intelligent retrieval of audiovisual files
- it will allow for observation and educated decision-taking on how one could proceed with mining the corpus or using it as training data for semantic multimedia processing applications, and
- it will allow interfacing with semantic lexical resources, computational lexicons, text processing components and cross-lingual information resources for automatically expanding and generalising the data (semantic relations) one can mine from the corpus.

We have developed such tool, the COSMOROE search interface. The interface itself is actually a text-based search engine, that indexes and retrieves information from the COSMOROE annotated corpus. The interface allows for both simple search and advanced search, depending on the type and needs of the users. The advanced search is designed for those who have a special interest in multimedia semantics and/or ones who want to develop systems that will be trained on the COSMOROE corpus. This advanced version allows search in a text-based manner, in either of these ways:

- Search using single or multiword query terms (keywords) that are mentioned in the *transcribed speech (or other text) of the video* or in the *visual labels set of its visual-units*, in order to find instantiations of different semantic relations in which they participate;
- Search using a *pair of single or multiword query terms* (keywords) that are related through (un)specified semantic relations;
- Search for specific *types of relations* and find out how these are realized through actual instances in a certain multimedia context;
- Search for specific *modality types* (e.g. specific types of gestures, image-regions etc.) and find out all the different relations in which they appear;

Figure 2 presents a search example, using the advanced interface[1]. The user has opted to search for all instances of the word "bell" appearing in the visual label of keyframe regions and/or video shots and in particular ones in which the bell is clearly shown either in the foreground or in the background. In a similar way, the user can search

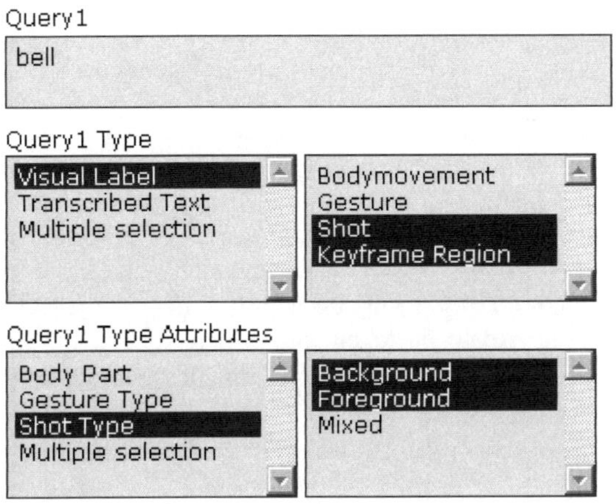

Figure 2: Search example

for concepts present in the audio part of the video, through the use of the "Transcribed Text" option or make a multiple selection. Another possibility is to use a "Query 2" set, in conjunction, disjunction or negation with "Query 1", in order to obtain the relations through which two categories of concepts are associated.

Multimedia relations can also be searched independently of their content, simply denoting the desired type. Finally, the user can search for special types of visual-units, such as body movements, gestures, images, without defining the concept they denote.

After executing the query, the user is presented with the list of the results, grouped by the semantic relation in which the visual labels —in the example case presented above— participate. Each hit is accompanied by its transcribed speech. Indication of the number of results found is given and the user has also the option to save the results of the specific search session. By clicking on individual hits in the result list, one may investigate the corresponding relation particulars.

Figure 3 shows such detailed view of one of the results of the query shown in Figure 2. All relation

Field	Value
Video	GT-Greece-B-EN.avi
Topic	Travel in Greece: Patmos
	Transcript
Utterance	One of the prettiest islands in the Aegean, Patmos is also seen as a sacred place to many Christians and there has been a monastery here since ten eighty eight.
	Anchor Text
Anchor Utterance Type	token
Anchor Utterance	monastery
	Shots
Shot	View video
Image Type	*background*
Shot Label	*bell* tower
	Keyframe Regions
Keyframe	
Keyframe Label	*bell*
	Relation
Relation File ID	relations/GT-Greece-B-EN_Equivalence_105.xml
Relation Type	equivalence
Relation First Level Subtype	figurative
Relation Second Level Subtype	metonymy
Relation Third Level Subtype	part for whole
Metonymy Direction	image language
Relation Video	View video

Figure 3: Example result - relation template

components are presented, textual and visual ones. There are links to the video file from which the relation comes, at the specified time offsets. Also, the user may watch the video clips of the modalities that participate in the relation (e.g. a particular gesture) and/or a static image (keyframe) of a participating image region (e.g. a specific object) with the contour of the object highlighted.

In this example, one may see that the word "monastery", which was mentioned in the transcribed speech of the file, is grounded to the video sequence depicting a "bell tower" in the background and to another image of a "bell", through a metonymic relation of type "part for whole". What is actually happening, from a semantic point of view, is that although the video talks about a "monastery", it never actually shows the building, it shows a characteristic part of it instead. In this page, the option to save these relation elements as a text file, is also provided.

Last, a user may get a *quantified profile* of the contents of the database (the annotated corpus) in terms of number of relations per type, per language, per file, or even per file producer, number of visual objects, gestures of different types, body

[1]Only part of the advanced search interface is depicted for the screenshot to be intelligible

movements, word tokens, visual labels, frequencies of such data per file/set of files, as well as co-occurrence statistics on word-visual label pairs per relation/file/language and other parameters.

For the novice or general user, a simple interface is provided that allows the user to submit a text query, with no other specifications. The results consist of a hit list with thumbnails of the video-clips related to the query and the corresponding transcribed utterance. Individual hits lead to full viewing of the video clip. Further details on the hit, i.e. information an advanced user would get, are available following the advance-information link. The use of semantic relations in multimedia data, in this case, is hidden in the way results are sorted in the results list. The sorting follows a highly to less informative pattern relying on whether the transcript words or visual labels matched to the query participate in cross-media relations or not, and in which relation. Automating the processing of audiovisual files for the extraction of cross-media semantics, in order to get this type of "intelligence" in search and retrieval within digital video archives, is the ultimate objective of the COSMOROE approach.

3.1 Technical Details

In developing the COSMOROE search interface, specific application needs had to be taken into consideration. The main goal was to develop a text-based search engine module capable of handling files in the .xml format and accessed by local and remote users. The core implementation is actually a web application, mainly based on the Apache Lucene[2] search engine library. This choice is supported by Lucene's intrinsic characteristics, such as high-performance indexing and searching, scalability and customization options and open source, cross-platform implementation, that render it one of the most suitable solutions for text-based search.

In particular, we exploited and further developed the built-in features of Lucene, in order to meet our design criteria:

- The relation specific .xml files were indexed in a way that retained their internal tree structure, while multilingual files can easily be handled during indexing and searching phases;
- The queries are formed in a text-like manner by the user, but are treated in a combined way by the system, that enables a relational search, enhanced with linguistic capabilities;
- The results are shown using custom sorting methods, making them more presentable and easily browsed by the user;
- Since Lucene is written in Java the application is basically platform-independent;
- The implementation of the Lucene search engine as a web application makes it easily accessible to local and remote users, through a simple web browser page.

During the results presentation phase, a special issue had to be taken into consideration, that is video sharing. Due to performance and security reasons, the Red5[3] server is used, which is an open source flash server, supporting secure streaming video.

4 Conclusion: towards computational modelling of multimedia dialectics

The COSMOROE search interface presented in this paper is the first phase for supporting the computational modelling of multimedia dialectics. The tool aims at providing a user-friendly access to the COSMOROE corpus, illustrating the theory through specific examples and providing an interface platform for reaching towards computational linguistic resources and tools that will generalise over the semantic information provided by the corpus. Last, the tool illustrates the hidden intelligence one could achieve with cross-media semantics in search engines of the future.

References

K. Pastra. 2008. Cosmoroe: A cross-media relations framework for modelling multimedia dialectics. *Multimedia Systems*, 14:299–323.

E. Rosch. 1978. Principles of categorization. In E. Rosch and B. Lloyd, editors, *Cognition and Categorization*, chapter 2, pages 27–48. Lawrence Erlbaum Associates.

S. Whittaker and M. Walker. 1991. Toward a theory of multi-modal interaction. In *Proceedings of the National Conference on Artificial Intelligence Workshop on Multi-modal Interaction.*

[2] http://lucene.apache.org/

[3] http://osflash.org/red5/

Grammar Development in GF

Aarne Ranta and **Krasimir Angelov** and **Björn Bringert***
Department of Computer Science and Engineering
Chalmers University of Technology and University of Gothenburg
{aarne,krasimir,bringert}@chalmers.se

Abstract

GF is a grammar formalism that has a powerful type system and module system, permitting a high level of abstraction and division of labour in grammar writing. GF is suited both for expert linguists, who appreciate its capacity of generalizations and conciseness, and for beginners, who benefit from its static type checker and, in particular, the GF Resource Grammar Library, which currently covers 12 languages. GF has a notion of multilingual grammars, enabling code sharing, linguistic generalizations, rapid development of translation systems, and painless porting of applications to new languages.

1 Introduction

Grammar implementation for natural languages is a challenge for both linguistics and engineering. The linguistic challenge is to master the complexities of languages so that all details are taken into account and work seamlessly together; if possible, the description should be concise and elegant, and capture the linguist's generalizations on the level of code. The engineering challenge is to make the grammar scalable, reusable, and maintainable. Too many grammars implemented in the history of computational linguistics have become obsolete, not only because of their poor maintainability, but also because of the decay of entire software and hardware platforms.

The first measure to be taken against the "bit rot" of grammars is to write them in **well-defined formats** that can be implemented independently of platform. This requirement is more or less an axiom in programming language development: a language must have syntax and semantics specifications that are independent of its first implementation; otherwise the first implementation risks to remain the only one.

Secondly, since grammar engineering is to a large extent software engineering, grammar formalisms should learn from programming language techniques that have been found useful in this respect. Two such techniques are **static type systems** and **module systems**. Since grammar formalism implementations are mostly descendants of Lisp and Prolog, they usually lack a static type system that finds errors at compile time. In a complex task like grammar writing, compile-time error detection is preferable to run-time debugging whenever possible. As for modularity, traditional grammar formalisms again inherit from Lisp and Prolog low-level mechanisms like macros and file includes, which in modern languages like Java and ML have been replaced by advanced module systems akin in rigour to type systems.

Thirdly, as another lesson from software engineering, grammar writing should permit an increasing use of **libraries**, so that programmers can build on ealier code. Types and modules are essential for the management of libraries. When a new language is developed, an effort is needed in creating libraries for the language, so that programmers can scale up to real-size tasks.

Fourthly, a grammar formalism should have a **stable and efficient implementation** that works on different platforms (hardware and operating systems). Since grammars are often parts of larger language-processing systems (such as translation tools or dialogue systems), their **interoperability** with other components is an important issue. The implementation should provide compilers to standard formats, such as databases and speech recognition language models. In addition to interoperability, such compilers also help keeping the grammars alive even if the original grammar formalism

*Now at Google Inc.

Proceedings of the EACL 2009 Demonstrations Session, pages 57–60,
Athens, Greece, 3 April 2009. ©2009 Association for Computational Linguistics

ceases to exist.

Fifthly, grammar formalisms should have **rich documentation**; in particular, they should have accessible tutorials that do not demand the readers to be experts in a linguistic theory or in computer programming. Also the libraries should be documented, preferably by automatically generated documentation in the style of JavaDoc, which is guaranteed to stay up to date.

Last but not least, a grammar formalism, as well its documentation, implementation, and standard libraries, should be **freely available open-source software** that anyone can use, inspect, modify, and improve. In the domain of general-purpose programming, this is yet another growing trend; proprietary languages are being made open-source or at least free of charge.

2 The GF programming language

The development of GF started in 1998 at Xerox Research Centre Europe in Grenoble, within a project entitled "Multilingual Document Authoring" (Dymetman & al. 2000). Its purpose was to make it productive to build controlled-language translators and multilingual authoring systems, previously produced by hard-coded grammar rules rather than declarative grammar formalisms (Power & Scott 1998). Later, mainly at Chalmers University in Gothenburg, GF developed into a functional programming language inspired by ML and Haskell, with a strict type system and operational semantics specified in (Ranta 2004). A module system was soon added (Ranta 2007), inspired by the parametrized modules of ML and the class inheritance hierarchies of Java, although with multiple inheritance in the style of C++.

Technically, GF falls within the class of so-called Curry-style categorial grammars, inspired by the distinction between tectogrammatical and phenogrammatical structure in (Curry 1963). Thus a GF grammar has an **abstract syntax** defining a system of types and trees (i.e. a free algebra), and a **concrete syntax**, which is a homomorphic mapping from trees to strings and, more generally, to **records** of strings and features. To take a simple example, the NP-VP predication rule, written

```
S ::= NP VP
```

in a context-free notation, becomes in GF a pair of an abstract and a concrete syntax rule,

```
fun Pred : NP -> VP -> S
lin Pred np vp = np ++ vp
```

The keyword `fun` stands for function declaration (declaring the function `Pred` of type `NP -> VP -> S`), whereas `lin` stands for linearization (saying that trees of form `Pred np vp` are converted to strings where the linearization of `np` is followed by the linearization of `vp`). The arrow `->` is the normal function type arrow of programming languages, and ++ is concatenation.

Patterns more complex than string concatenation can be used in linearizations of the same predication trees as the rule above. Thus **agreement** can be expressed by using features passed from the noun phrase to the verb phrase. The noun phrase is here defined as not just a string, but as a record with two fields—a string `s` and an agreement feature `a`. Verb-subject inversion can be expressed by making VP into a **discontinuous constituent**, i.e. a record with separate verb and complement fields `v` and `c`. Combining these two phenomena, we write

```
vp.v ! np.a ++ np.s ++ vp.c
```

(For the details of the notation, we refer to documentation on the GF web page.) Generalizing strings into richer data structures makes it smooth to deal accurately with complexities such as German constituent order and Romance clitics, while maintaining the simple tree structure defined by the abstract syntax of `Pred`.

Separating abstract and concrete syntax makes it possible to write **multilingual grammars**, where one abstract syntax is equipped with several concrete syntaxes. Thus different string configurations can be mapped into the same abstract syntax trees. For instance, the distinction between SVO and VSO languages can be ignored on the abstract level, and so can all other {S,V,O} patterns as well. Also the differences in feature systems can be abstracted away from. For instance, agreement features in English are much simpler than in Arabic; yet the same abstract syntax can be used.

Since concrete syntax is reversible between linearization and parsing (Ljunglöf 2004), multilingual grammars can be used for **translation**, where the abstract syntax works as interlingua. Experience from translation projects (e.g. Burke and Johannisson 2005, Caprotti 2006) has shown that the interlingua-based translation provided by GF gives good quality in domain-specific tasks. However, GF also supports the use of a transfer component if the compositional method implied by multilingual grammars does not suffice (Bringert and Ranta

2008). The language-theoretical strenght of GF is between mildly and fully context-sensitive, with polynomial parsing complexity (Ljunglöf 2004).

In addition to multilingual grammars, GF is usable for more traditional, large-scale unilingual grammar development. The "middle-scale" resource grammars can be extended to wide-coverage grammars, by adding a few rules and a large lexicon. GF provides powerful tools for building morphological lexica and exporting them to other formats, including Xerox finite state tools (Beesley and Karttunen 2003) and SQL databases (Forsberg and Ranta 2004). Some large lexica have been ported to the GF format from freely available sources for Bulgarian, English, Finnish, Hindi, and Swedish, comprising up to 70,000 lemmas and over two million word forms.

3 The GF Resource Grammar Library

The GF Resource Grammar Library is a comprehensive multilingual grammar currently implemented for 12 languages: Bulgarian, Catalan, Danish, English, Finnish, French, German, Italian, Norwegian, Russian, Spanish, and Swedish. Work is in progress on Arabic, Hindi/Urdu, Latin, Polish, Romanian, and Thai. The library is an open-source project, which constantly attracts new contributions.

The library can be seen as an experiment on how far the notion of multilingual grammars extends and how GF scales up to wide-coverage grammars. Its primary purpose, however, is to provide a programming resource similar to the standard libraries of various programming languages. When all linguistic details are taken into account, grammar writing is an expert programming task, and the library aims to make this expertise available to non-expert application programmers.

The coverage of the library is comparable to the Core Language Engine (Rayner & al. 2000). It has been developed and tested in applications ranging from a translation system for software specifications (Burke and Johannisson 2005) to in-car dialogue systems (Perera and Ranta 2007).

The use of a grammar as a library is made possible by the type and module system of GF (Ranta 2007). What is more, the API (Application Programmer's Interface) of the library is to a large extent language-independent. For instance, an NP-VP predication rule is available for all languages, even though the underlying details of predication vary greatly from one language to another.

A typical domain grammar, such as the one in Perera and Ranta (2007), has 100–200 syntactic combinations and a lexicon of a few hundred lemmas. Building the syntax with the help of the library is a matter of a few working days. Once it is built for one language, porting it to other languages mainly requires writing the lexicon. By the use of the inflection libraries, this is a matter of hours. Thus porting a domain grammar to a new language requires very effort and also very little linguistic knowledge: it is expertise of the application domain and its terminology that is needed.

4 The GF grammar compiler

The GF grammar compiler is usable in two ways: in batch mode, and as an interactive shell. The shell is a useful tool for developers as it provides testing facilities such as parsing, linerization, random generation, and grammar statistics. Both modes use PGF, **Portable Grammar Format**, which is the "machine language" of GF permitting fast run-time linearization and parsing (Angelov & al. 2008). PGF interpreters have been written in C++, Java, and Haskell, permitting an easy embedding of grammars in systems written in these languages. PGF can moreover be translated to other formats, including language models for speech recognition (e.g. Nuance and HTK; see Bringert 2007a), VoiceXML (Bringert 2007b), and JavaScript (Meza Moreno and Bringert 2008). The grammar compiler is heavily optimizing, so that the use of a large library grammar in small run-time applications produces no penalty.

For the working grammarian, static type checking is maybe the most unique feature of the GF grammar compiler. Type checking does not only detect errors in grammars. It also enables aggressive optimizations (type-driven partial evaluation), and **overloading resolution**, which makes it possible to use the same name for different functions whose types are different.

5 Related work

As a grammar development system, GF is comparable to Regulus (Rayner 2006), LKB (Copestake 2002), and XLE (Kaplan and Maxwell 2007). The unique features of GF are its type and module system, support for multilingual grammars, the large number of back-end formats, and the availability of libraries for 12 languages. Regulus has resource grammars for 7 languages, but they are smaller in scope. In LKB, the LinGO grammar matrix has been developed for several languages (Bender and Flickinger 2005), and in XLE, the Pargram grammar set (Butt & al. 2002). LKB and XLE tools have been targeted to linguists working with large-scale grammars, rather than for general programmers working with applications.

References

[Angelov et al.2008] K. Angelov, B. Bringert, and A. Ranta. 2008. PGF: A Portable Run-Time Format for Type-Theoretical Grammars. Chalmers University. Submitted for publication.

[Beesley and Karttunen2003] K. Beesley and L. Karttunen. 2003. *Finite State Morphology*. CSLI Publications.

[Bender and Flickinger2005] Emily M. Bender and Dan Flickinger. 2005. Rapid prototyping of scalable grammars: Towards modularity in extensions to a language-independent core. In *Proceedings of the 2nd International Joint Conference on Natural Language Processing IJCNLP-05 (Posters/Demos)*, Jeju Island, Korea.

[Bringert and Ranta2008] B. Bringert and A. Ranta. 2008. A Pattern for Almost Compositional Functions. *The Journal of Functional Programming*, 18(5–6):567–598.

[Bringert2007a] B. Bringert. 2007a. Speech Recognition Grammar Compilation in Grammatical Framework. In *SPEECHGRAM 2007: ACL Workshop on Grammar-Based Approaches to Spoken Language Processing, June 29, 2007, Prague*.

[Bringert2007b] Björn Bringert. 2007b. Rapid Development of Dialogue Systems by Grammar Compilation. In Simon Keizer, Harry Bunt, and Tim Paek, editors, *Proceedings of the 8th SIGdial Workshop on Discourse and Dialogue, Antwerp, Belgium*, pages 223–226. Association for Computational Linguistics, September.

[Bringert2008] B. Bringert. 2008. Semantics of the GF Resource Grammar Library. Report, Chalmers University.

[Burke and Johannisson2005] D. A. Burke and K. Johannisson. 2005. Translating Formal Software Specifications to Natural Language / A Grammar-Based Approach. In P. Blache and E. Stabler and J. Busquets and R. Moot, editor, *Logical Aspects of Computational Linguistics (LACL 2005)*, volume 3492 of *LNCS/LNAI*, pages 51–66. Springer.

[Butt et al.2002] M. Butt, H. Dyvik, T. Holloway King, H. Masuichi, and C. Rohrer. 2002. The Parallel Grammar Project. In *COLING 2002, Workshop on Grammar Engineering and Evaluation*, pages 1–7. URL

[Caprotti2006] O. Caprotti. 2006. WebALT! Deliver Mathematics Everywhere. In *Proceedings of SITE 2006. Orlando March 20-24*.

[Copestake2002] A. Copestake. 2002. *Implementing Typed Feature Structure Grammars*. CSLI Publications.

[Curry1963] H. B. Curry. 1963. Some logical aspects of grammatical structure. In Roman Jakobson, editor, *Structure of Language and its Mathematical Aspects: Proceedings of the Twelfth Symposium in Applied Mathematics*, pages 56–68. American Mathematical Society.

[Dymetman et al.2000] M. Dymetman, V. Lux, and A. Ranta. 2000. XML and multilingual document authoring: Convergent trends. In *COLING, Saarbrücken, Germany*, pages 243–249.

[Forsberg and Ranta2004] M. Forsberg and A. Ranta. 2004. Functional Morphology. In *ICFP 2004, Showbird, Utah*, pages 213–223.

[Ljunglöf2004] P. Ljunglöf. 2004. *The Expressivity and Complexity of Grammatical Framework*. Ph.D. thesis, Dept. of Computing Science, Chalmers University of Technology and Gothenburg University.

[Meza Moreno and Bringert2008] M. S. Meza Moreno and B. Bringert. 2008. Interactive Multilingual Web Applications with Grammarical Framework. In B. Nordström and A. Ranta, editors, *Advances in Natural Language Processing (GoTAL 2008)*, volume 5221 of *LNCS/LNAI*, pages 336–347.

[Perera and Ranta2007] N. Perera and A. Ranta. 2007. Dialogue System Localization with the GF Resource Grammar Library. In *SPEECHGRAM 2007: ACL Workshop on Grammar-Based Approaches to Spoken Language Processing, June 29, 2007, Prague*.

[Power and Scott1998] R. Power and D. Scott. 1998. Multilingual authoring using feedback texts. In *COLING-ACL*.

[Ranta2004] A. Ranta. 2004. Grammatical Framework: A Type-Theoretical Grammar Formalism. *The Journal of Functional Programming*, 14(2):145–189.

[Ranta2007] A. Ranta. 2007. Modular Grammar Engineering in GF. *Research on Language and Computation*, 5:133–158.

[Rayner et al.2000] M. Rayner, D. Carter, P. Bouillon, V. Digalakis, and M. Wirén. 2000. *The Spoken Language Translator*. Cambridge University Press, Cambridge.

[Rayner et al.2006] M. Rayner, B. A. Hockey, and P. Bouillon. 2006. *Putting Linguistics into Speech Recognition: The Regulus Grammar Compiler*. CSLI Publications.

Three BioNLP Tools Powered by a Biological Lexicon

Yutaka Sasaki [1] **Paul Thompson**[1] **John McNaught** [1, 2] **Sophia Ananiadou**[1, 2]

[1] School of Computer Science, University of Manchester
[2] National Centre for Text Mining
MIB, 131 Princess Street, Manchester, M1 7DN, United Kingdom
{Yutaka.Sasaki,Paul.Thompson,John.McNaught,Sophia.Ananiadou}@manchester.ac.uk

Abstract

In this paper, we demonstrate three NLP applications of the BioLexicon, which is a lexical resource tailored to the biology domain. The applications consist of a dictionary-based POS tagger, a syntactic parser, and query processing for biomedical information retrieval. Biological terminology is a major barrier to the accurate processing of literature within biology domain. In order to address this problem, we have constructed the BioLexicon using both manual and semi-automatic methods. We demonstrate the utility of the biology-oriented lexicon within three separate NLP applications.

1 Introduction

Processing of biomedical text can frequently be problematic, due to the huge number of technical terms and idiosyncratic usages of those terms. Sometimes, general English words are used in different ways or with different meanings in biology literature.

There are a number of linguistic resources that can be use to improve the quality of biological text processing. WordNet (Fellbaum, 1998) and the NLP Specialist Lexicon [1] are dictionaries commonly used within biomedical NLP.

WordNet is a general English thesaurus which additionally covers biological terms. However, since WordNet is not targeted at the biology domain, many biological terms and derivational relations are missing.

The Specialist Lexicon is a syntactic lexicon of biomedical and general English words, providing linguistic information about individual vocabulary items (Browne *et al.*, 2003). Whilst it contains a large number of biomedical terms, its focus is on medical terms. Therefore some biology-specific terms, *e.g.*, molecular biology terms, are not the main target of the lexicon.

In response to this, we have constructed the BioLexicon (Sasaki *et al.*, 2008), a lexical resource tailored to the biology domain. We will demonstrate three applications of the BioLexicon, in order to illustrate the utility of the lexicon within the biomedical NLP field.

The three applications are:

- BLTagger: a dictionary-based POS tagger based on the BioLexicon
- Enju full parser enriched by the BioLexicon
- Lexicon-based query processing for information retrieval

2. Summary of the BioLexicon

In this section, we provide a summary of the BioLexicon (Sasaki *et al.*, 2008). It contains words belonging to four part-of-speech categories: verb, noun, adjective, and adverb.

Quochi *et al.*(2008) designed the database model of the BioLexicon which follows the Lexical Markup Framework (Francopoulo *et al.*, 2008).

2.1 Entries in the Biology Lexicon

The BioLexicon accommodates both general English words and terminologies. Biomedical terms were gathered from existing biomedical databases. Detailed information regarding the sources of biomedical terms can be found in (Rebholz-Schuhmann *et al.*, 2008). The lexicon entries consist of the following:

(1) Terminological verbs: 759 base forms (4,556 inflections) of terminological verbs with automatically extracted verb subcategorization frames

[1] http://SPECIALIST.nlm.hih.gov

Proceedings of the EACL 2009 Demonstrations Session, pages 61–64,
Athens, Greece, 3 April 2009. ©2009 Association for Computational Linguistics

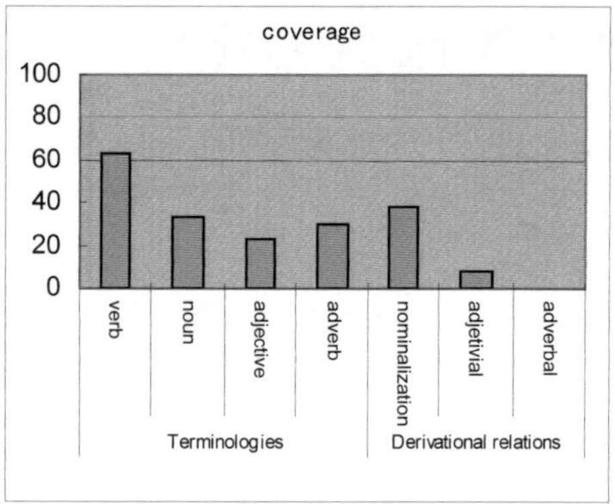

Fig. 1 Comparison with WordNet

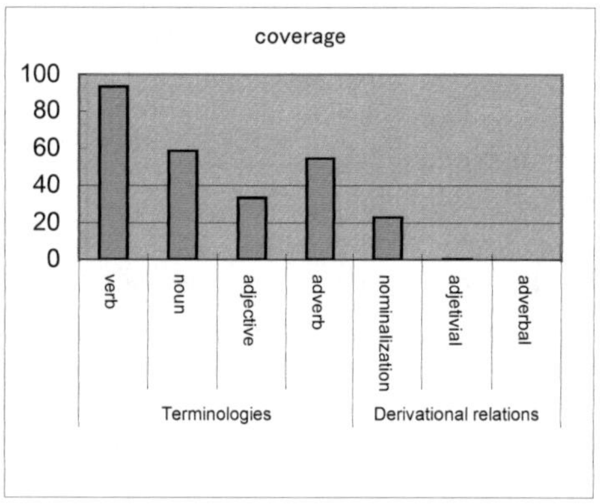

Fig. 2 Comparison with Specialist Lexicon

(2)Terminological adjectives: 1,258 terminological adjectives.
(3) Terminological adverbs: 130 terminological adverbs.
(4) Nominalized verbs: 1,771 nominalized verbs.
(5) Biomedical terms: Currently, the BioLexicon contains biomedical terms in the categories of cell (842 entries, 1,400 variants), chemicals (19,637 entries, 106,302 variants), enzymes (4,016 entries, 11,674 variants), diseases (19,457 entries, 33,161 variants), genes and proteins (1,640,608 entries, 3,048,920 variants), gene ontology concepts (25,219 entries, 81,642 variants), molecular role concepts (8,850 entries, 60,408 variants), operons (2,672 entries, 3,145 variants), protein complexes (2,104 entries, 2,647 variants), protein domains (16,940 entries, 33,880 variants), Sequence ontology concepts (1,431 entries, 2,326 variants), species (482,992 entries, 669,481 variants), and transcription factors (160 entries, 795 variants).

In addition to the existing gene/protein names, 70,105 variants of gene/protein names have been newly extracted from 15 million MEDLINE abstracts. (Sasaki *et al.*, 2008)

2.2. Comparison to existing lexicons

This section focuses on the words and derivational relations of words that are covered by our BioLexicon but not by comparable existing resources. Figures 1 and 2 show the percentage of the terminological words and derivational relations (such as the word *retroregulate* and the derivational relation *retroregulate* → *retroregulation*) in our lexicon that are also found in WorNet and the Specialist Lexicion.

Since WordNet is not targeted at the biology domain, many biological terms and derivational relations are not included.

Because the Specialist Lexicon is a biomedical lexicon and the target is broader than our lexicon, some biology-oriented words and relations are missing. For example, the Specialist Lexicon includes the term *retro-regulator* but not *retro-regulate.* This means that derivational relations of *retro-regulate* are not covered by the Specialist Lexicon.

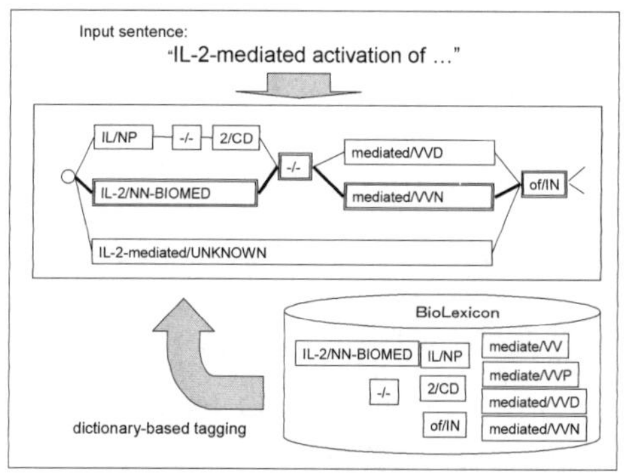

Fig. 3 BLTagger example

3. Application 1: BLTagger

Dictionary-based POS tagging is advantageous when a sentence contains technical terms that conflict with general English words. If the POS tags are decided without considering possible occurrences of biomedical terms, then POS errors could arise.

For example, in the protein name "met proto-oncogene precursor", *met* might be incorrectly recognized as a verb by a non dictionary-based tagger.

In the dictionary, biomedical terms are given POS tag "NN-BIOMED". Given a sentence, the dictionary-based POS tagger works as follows.

- Find all word sequences that match the lexical entries, and create a token graph (*i.e.*, trellis) according to the word order.
- Estimate the score of every path using the weights of the nodes and edges, through training using Conditional Random Fields.
- Select the best path.

Figure 3 shows an example of our dictionary-based POS tagger BLTagger.

Suppose that the input is "IL-2-mediated activation of". A trellis is created based on the lexical entries in the dictionary. The selection criteria for the best path are determined by the CRF tagging model trained on the Genia corpus (Kim *et al.*, 2003). In this example,

```
IL-2/NN-BIOMED -/- mediated/VVN
activation/NN of/IN
```

is selected as the best path.

Following Kudo et al. (2004), we adapted the core engine of the CRF-based morphological analyzer, MeCab[2], to our POS tagging task.

The features used were:

- *POS*
- `BIOMED`
- *POS*-`BIOMED`
- bigram of adjacent *POS*
- bigram of adjacent `BIOMED`
- bigram of adjacent *POS*-`BIOMED`

During the construction of the trellis, white space is considered as the delimiter unless otherwise stated within dictionary entries. This means that unknown tokens are character sequences without spaces.

As the BioLexicon associates biomedical semantic IDs with terms, the BLTagger attaches semantic IDs to the tokenizing/tagging results.

4. Application 2: Enju full parser with the BioLexicon

Enju (Miyao, *et al.*, 2003) is an HPSG parser, which is tuned to the biomedical domain. Sentences are parsed based on the output of the Stepp POS tagger, which is also tuned to the biomedical domain.

To further tune Enju to the biology domain, (especially molecular biology), we have modified Enju to parse sentences based on the output of the BLTagger.

As the BioLexicon contains many multi-word biological terms, the modified version of Enju parses token sequences in which some of the tokens are multi-word expressions. This is effective when very long technical terms (*e.g.*, more than 20 words) are present in a sentence.

To use the dictionary-based tagging for parsing, unknown words should be avoided as much as possible. In order to address this issue, we added entries in WordNet and the Specialist Lexicion to the dictionary of BLTagger.

The enhancement in the performance of Enju based on these changes is still under evaluation. However, we demonstrate a functional, modified version of Enju.

5. Application 3: Query processing for IR

It is sometimes the case that queries for biomedical IR systems contain long technical terms that should be handled as single multi-word expressions.

We have applied BLTagger to the TREC 2007 Genomics Track data (Hersh *et al.*, 2007). The goal of the TREC Genomics Track 2007 was to generate a ranked list of passages for 36 queries that relate to biological events and processes.

Firstly, we processed the documents with a conventional tokenizer and standard stop-word remover, and then created an index containing the words in the documents. Queries are processed with the BLTagger and multi-word expressions are used as phrase queries. Passages are ranked with Okapi BM25 (Robertson *et al.*, 1995).

Table 1 shows the preliminary Mean Average Precision (MAP) scores of applying the BLTagger to the TREC data set.

By adding biology multi-word expressions identified by the BLTagger to query terms (row (a)), we were able to obtain a slightly better Passage2 score. As the BLTagger outputs semantic IDs which are defined in the BioLexicon, we tried to use these semantic IDs for query expansion (rows (b) and (d)). However, the MAP scores degraded.

[2] http://sourceforge.net/project/showfiles.php?group id=177856/

Table 1 Preliminary MAP scores for TREC Genomics Track 2007 data

Query expansion method	Passage2 MAP	Aspect MAP	Document MAP
(a) BioLexicon terms	0.0702	0.1726	0.2158
(b) BioLexicon terms + semantic IDs	0.0696	0.1673	0.2148
(c) no query expansion (baseline)	0.0683	0.1726	0.2183
(d) semantic IDs	0.0677	0.1670	0.2177

6. Conclusions

We have demonstrated three applications of the BioLexicon, which is a resource comprising linguistic information, targeted for use within bio-text mining applications.

We have described the following three applications that will be useful for processing of biological literature.

- BLTagger: dictionary-based POS tagger based on the BioLexicon
- Enju full parser enriched by the BioLexicon
- Lexicon-based query processing for information retrieval

Our future work will include further intrinsic and extrinsic evaluations of the BioLexicon in NLP, including its application to information extraction tasks in the biology domain. The BioLexicon is available for non-commercial purposes under the Creative Commons license.

Acknowledgements

This research has been supported by the EC IST project FP6-028099 (BOOTStrep), whose Manchester team is hosted by the JISC/BBSRC/EPSRC sponsored National Centre for Text Mining.

References

Browne, A.C., G. Divita, A.R. Aronson, and A.T. McCray. 2003. UMLS Language and Vocabulary Tools. In *Proc. of AMIA Annual Symposium 2003*, p.798.

Dietrich Rebholz-Schuhmann, Piotr Pezik, Vivian Lee, Jung-Jae Kim, Riccardo del Gratta, Yutaka Sasaki, Jock McNaught, Simonetta Montemagni, Monica Monachini, Nicoletta Calzolari, Sophia Ananiadou, BioLexicon: Towards a Reference Terminological Resource in the Biomedical Domain, *the 16th Annual International Conference on Intelligent Systems for Molecular Biology (ISMB-2008)* (Poster), Toronto, Canada, 2008. http://www.ebi.ac.uk/Rebholz-srv/BioLexicon/BioLexicon_Poster_EBI_UoM_ILC.pdf)

Fellbaum, C., editor. 1998. *WordNet: An Electronic Lexical Database*. MIT Press, Cambridge, MA..

Francopoulo, G., M. George, N. Calzolari, M. Monachini, N. Bel, M. Pet, and C. Soria. 2006. Lexical Markup Framework (LMF). In *Proc. of LREC 2006*, Genova, Italy.

Hersh, W., Aaron Cohen, Lynn Ruslen, and Phoebe Roberts, TREC 2007 Genomics Track Overview, *TREC-2007*, 2007.

Kim, J-D., T. Ohta, Y. Tateisi, and J. Tsujii. 2003. GENIA Corpus - Semantically Annotated Corpus for Bio-Text Mining. *Bioinformatics*, 19:i180-i182.

Kudo T., Yamamoto K., Matsumoto Y., Applying Conditional Random Fields to Japanese Morphological Analysis. In *Proc. of Empirical Methods in Natural Language Processing (EMNLP-04)*, pp. 230–237, 2004.

Lafferty, J., A. McCallum, and F. Pereira. 2001. Conditional Random Fields: Probabilistic Models for Segmenting and Labelling Sequence Data. In *Proc. of the Eighteenth International Conference on Machine Learning (ICML-2001),* pages 282-289.

Miyao, Y. and J. Tsujii, 2003. Probabilistic modeling of argument structures including non-local dependencies. In *Proc. of the Conference on Recent Advances in Natural Language Processing (RANLP 2003)*, pages 285-291.

Quochi, V., Monachini, M., Del Gratta, R., Calzolari, N., A lexicon for biology and bioinformatics: the BOOTStrep experience. In *Proc. of LREC 2008*, Marrakech, 2008.

Robertson, S.E., Walker S., Jones, S., Hancock-Beaulieu M.M., and Gatford, M., 1995. Okapi at TREC-3. In *Proc of Overview of the Third Text REtrieval Conference (TREC-3)*, pp. 109–126.

Yutaka Sasaki, Simonetta Montemagni, Piotr Pezik, Dietrich Rebholz-Schuhmann, John McNaught, and Sophia Ananiadou, BioLexicon: A Lexical Resource for the Biology Domain, In *Proc. of the Third International Symposium on Semantic Mining in Biomedicine (SMBM 2008)*, 2008.

A Mobile Health and Fitness Companion Demonstrator*

Olov Ståhl[1] **Björn Gambäck**[1,2] **Markku Turunen**[3] **Jaakko Hakulinen**[3]

[1]ICE / Userware
Swedish Inst. of Computer Science
Kista, Sweden
{olovs,gamback}@sics.se

[2]Dpt. Computer & Information Science
Norwegian Univ. of Science and Technology
Trondheim, Norway
gamback@idi.ntnu.no

[3]Dpt. Computer Sciences
Univ. of Tampere
Tampere, Finland
{mturunen,jh}@cs.uta.fi

Abstract

Multimodal conversational spoken dialogues using physical and virtual agents provide a potential interface to motivate and support users in the domain of health and fitness. The paper presents a multimodal conversational Companion system focused on health and fitness, which has both a stationary and a mobile component.

Figure 1: H&F Companion Architecture

1 Introduction

Spoken dialogue systems have traditionally focused on task-oriented dialogues, such as making flight bookings or providing public transport timetables. In emerging areas, such as domain-oriented dialogues (Dybkjaer et al., 2004), the interaction with the system, typically modelled as a conversation with a virtual anthropomorphic character, can be the main motivation for the interaction. Recent research has coined the term "Companions" to describe embodied multimodal conversational agents having a long lasting interaction history with their users (Wilks, 2007).

Such a conversational Companion within the Health and Fitness (H&F) domain helps its users to a healthier lifestyle. An H&F Companion has quite different motivations for use than traditional task-based spoken dialogue systems. Instead of helping with a single, well-defined task, it truly aims to be a Companion to the user, providing social support in everyday activities. The system should thus be a peer rather than act as an expert system in health-related issues. It is important to stress that it is the Companion concept which is central, rather than the fitness area as such. Thus it is not of vital importance that the system should be a first-rate fitness coach, but it is essential that it should be able to take a persistent part in the user's life, that is, that it should be able to follow the user in all the user's activities. This means that the Companion must have mobile capabilities. Not necessarily self-mobile (as a robot), but allowing the user to bring the system with her, like a handbag or a pair of shoes — or as a mobile phone.

The paper describes such a Health and Fitness Companion. It has a stationary ("home") component accounting for the main part of the user interaction and a mobile component which follows the users in actual exercise activities. Section 2 outlines the overall system and its two basic components, and Section 3 details the implementation. Section 4 discusses some related work, while Section 5 describes the demonstrator set-up and plans for future work.

2 The Health and Fitness Companion

The overall system architecture of the Health and Fitness Companion is shown in Figure 1. The system components communicate with each other over a regular mobile phone network. The home system provides an exercise plan to the mobile part and in return gets the results of the performed exercises from the mobile component.

*The work was funded by the European Commission's IST priority through the project COMPANIONS (www.companions-project.org).

Figure 2: Home Companion interface

2.1 The Home H&F Companion

The home part of the H&F Companion gathers information from the user and makes suggestions targeted for a healthy lifestyle on a daily basis. The Companion communicates with the user in two main dialogue phases: a planning phase where the system talks about the coming day with the user and a reporting phase where the user's actual activities are assessed with reference to what was agreed on earlier. The Companion can discuss the following topics: travelling to work, getting lunch, activities to be performed before dinner, getting dinner, and activities to be performed after dinner. It knows activities such as playing football, squash, or badminton; going to the gym or shopping; and watching television or reading a book.

The Home Companion interface, illustrated in Figure 2, uses a Nabaztag/tag WLAN rabbit (`www.nabaztag.com`) as the physical agent interface. The Nabaztag rabbit provides audio output and push-to-talk speech input, moves its ears, and operates four coloured lights to signal its status. In the current implementation, the user needs to push the button located on top of the Nabaztag/tag device in order to speak to it. As an alternative, the system supports external micro-phones and loudspeakers. The user is also able to pick a topic by showing RFID tags (embedded in picture cards or other objects).

The following dialogue example demonstrates the interaction with the Companion.

```
C1: Do you have anything arranged for today?
U1: I'm playing Squash
C2: Is that before dinner?
U2: Yes
C3: Okay. Are you going to get the train to work?
U3: Yes
C4: Right. Could you take in a packed lunch to work?
U4: Yes, that would be fine
```

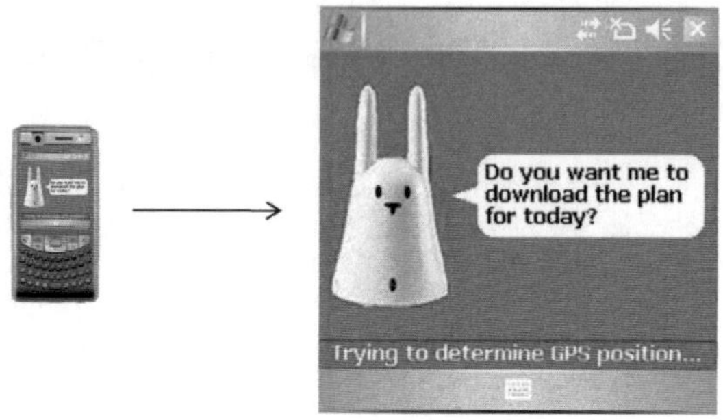

Figure 3: The Mobile Companion GUI

(Later on in the evening)

```
C6: Welcome back! How did your game of Squash go?
U5: The game was cancelled, so I went to the gym
C7: Okay. Did you take the train to work?
U6: Yes, I did
C8: Right. Did you take in a packed lunch?
U7: No. I was in a rush so I went to the cafeteria
```

2.2 The Mobile H&F Companion

The mobile part of the H&F Companion runs on a mobile handset (e.g., a PDA), and is used during physical exercise (e.g., while running or walking) to track the distance, pace, duration, and calories burned. The data gathered during an exercise is stored in the device's record store, and can be used to compare the results to previous runs.

The user interface of the Mobile Companion consists of a single screen showing an image of a Nabaztag rabbit along with some text areas where various exercise and device status information is displayed (Figure 3). The rabbit image is intended to give users a sense of communicating with the same Companion, no matter if they are using the home or mobile system. To further the feeling of persistence, the home and mobile parts of the H&F Companion also use the same TTS voice.

When the mobile Companion is started, it asks the user whether it should connect to the home system and download the current plan. Such a plan consists of various tasks (e.g., shopping or exercise tasks) that the user should try to achieve during the day, and is generated by the home system during a session with the user. If the user chooses to download the plan the Companion summarizes the content of the plan for the user, excluding all tasks that do not involve some kind of exercise activity. The Companion then suggests a suitable task based on time of day and the user's current location. If the user chooses not to download the plan, or rejects the suggested exercise(s), the Companion instead asks the user to suggest an exercise.

Once an exercise has been agreed upon, the Companion asks the user to start the exercise and will then track the progress (distances travelled, time, pace and calories burned) using a built-in GPS receiver. While exercising, the user can ask the Companion to play music or to give reports on how the user is doing. After the exercise, the Companion will summarize the result and up-load it to the Home system so it can be referred to later on.

3 H&F Companion Implementation

This section details the actual implementation of the Health and Fitness Companion, in terms of its two components (the home and mobile parts).

3.1 Home Companion Implementation

The Home Companion is implemented on top of Jaspis, a generic agent-based architecture designed for adaptive spoken dialogue systems (Turunen et al., 2005). The base architecture is extended to support interaction with virtual and physical Companions, in particular with the Nabaztag/tag device.

For speech inputs and outputs, the Home Companion uses Loquendo™ASR and TTS components. ASR grammars are in "Speech Recognition Grammar Specification" (W3C) format and include semantic tags in "Semantic Interpretation for Speech Recognition (SISR) Version 1.0" (W3C) format. Domain specific grammars were derived from a WoZ corpus. The grammars are dynamically selected according to the current dialogue state. Grammars can be precompiled for efficiency or compiled at run-time when dynamic grammar generation takes place in certain situations. The current system vocabulary consists of about 1400 words and a total of 900 CFG grammar rules in 60 grammars. Statistical language models for the system are presently being implemented.

Language understanding relies heavily on SISR information: given the current dialogue state, the input is parsed into a logical notation compatible with the planning implemented in a Cognitive Model. Additionally, a reduced set of DAMSL (Core and Allen, 1997) tags is used to mark functional dialogue acts using rule-based reasoning.

Language generation is implemented as a combination of canned utterances and tree adjoining grammar-based structures. The starting point for generation is predicate-form descriptions provided by the dialogue manager. Further details and contextual information are retrieved from the dialogue history and the user model. Finally, SSML (Speech Synthesis Markup Language) 1.0 tags are used for controlling the Loquendo synthesizer.

Dialogue management is based on close-cooperation of the Dialogue Manager and the Cognitive Manager. The Cognitive Manager models the domain, i.e., knows what to recommend to the user, what to ask from the user, and what kind of feedback to provide on domain level issues. In contrast, the Dialogue Manager focuses on interaction level phenomena, such as confirmations, turn taking, and initiative management.

The physical agent interface is implemented in jNabServer software to handle communication with Nabaztag/tags, that is, Wi-Fi enabled robotic rabbits. A Nabaztag/tag device can handle various forms of interaction, from voice to touch (button press), and from RFID 'sniffing' to ear movements. It can respond by moving its ears, or by displaying or changing the colour of its four LED lights. The rabbit can also play sounds such as music, synthesized speech, and other audio.

3.2 Mobile Companion Implementation

The Mobile Companion runs on Windows Mobile-based devices, such as the Fujitsu Siemens Pocket LOOX T830. The system is made up of two programs, both running on the mobile device: a Java midlet controls the main application logic (exercise tracking, dialogue management, etc.) as well as the graphical user interface; and a C++-based speech server that performs TTS and ASR functions on request by the Java midlet, such as loading grammar files or voices.

The midlet is made up of Java manager classes that provide basic services (event dispatching, GPS input, audio play-back, TTS and ASR, etc.). However, the main application logic and the GUI are implemented using scripts in the Hecl scripting language (`www.hecl.org`). The script files are read from the device's file system and evaluated in a script interpreter created by the midlet when started. The scripts have access to a number of commands, allowing them to initiate TTS and ASR operations, etc. Furthermore, events produced by the Java code are dispatched to the scripts, such as the user's current GPS position, GUI interactions (e.g., stylus interaction and button presses), and voice input. Scripts are also used to control the dialogue with the user.

The speech server is based on the Loquendo Embedded ASR (speaker-independent) and TTS software.[1] The Mobile Companion uses SRGS 1.0 grammars that are pre-compiled before being installed on the mobile device. The current system vocabulary consists of about 100 words in 10 dynamically selected grammars.

4 Related Work

As pointed out in the introduction, it is not the aim of the Health and Fitness Companion system to be a full-fledged fitness coach. There are several examples of commercial systems that aim to do that, e.g., miCoach (`www.micoach.com`) from Adidas and NIKE+ (`www.nike.com/nikeplus`).

MOPET (Buttussi and Chittaro, 2008) is a PDA-based personal trainer system supporting outdoor fitness activities. MOPET is similar to a Companion in that it tries to build a relationship with the user, but there is no real dialogue between the user and the system and it does not support speech input or output. Neither does MPTrain/TripleBeat (Oliver and Flores-Mangas, 2006; de Oliveira and Oliver, 2008), a system that runs on a mobile phone and aims to help users to more easily achieve their exercise goals. This is done by selecting music indicating the desired pace and different ways to enhance user motivation, but without an agent user interface model.

InCA (Kadous and Sammut, 2004) is a spoken language-based distributed personal assistant conversational character with a 3D avatar and facial animation. Similar to the Mobile Companion, the architecture is made up of a GUI client running on a PDA and a speech server, but the InCA server runs as a back-end system, while the Companion utilizes a stand-alone speech server.

5 Demonstration and Future Work

The demonstration will consist of two sequential interactions with the H&F Companion. First, the user and the home system will agree on a plan, consisting of various tasks that the user should try to achieve during the day. Then the mobile system will download the plan, and the user will have a dialogue with the Companion, concerning the selection of a suitable exercise activity, which the user will pretend to carry out.

Plans for future work include extending the mobile platform with various sensors, for example, a pulse sensor that gives the Companion information about the user's pulse while exercising, which can be used to provide feedback such as telling the user to speed up or slow down. We are also interested in using sensors to allow users to provide gesture-like input, in addition to the voice and button/screen click input available today.

Another modification we are considering is to unify the two dialogue management solutions currently used by the home and the mobile components into one. This would cause the Companion to "behave" more consistently in its two shapes, and make future extensions of the dialogue and the Companion behaviour easier to manage.

References

Fabio Buttussi and Luca Chittaro. 2008. MOPET: A context-aware and user-adaptive wearable system for fitness training. *Artificial Intelligence in Medicine*, 42(2):153–163.

Mark G. Core and James F. Allen. 1997. Coding dialogs with the DAMSL annotation scheme. In *AAAI Fall Symposium on Communicative Action in Humans and Machines*, pages 28–35, Cambridge, Massachusetts.

Laila Dybkjaer, Niels Ole Bernsen, and Wolfgang Minker. 2004. Evaluation and usability of multimodal spoken language dialogue systems. *Speech Communication*, 43(1-2):33–54.

Mohammed Waleed Kadous and Claude Sammut. 2004. InCa: A mobile conversational agent. In *Proceedings of the 8th Pacific Rim International Conference on Artificial Intelligence*, pages 644–653, Auckland, New Zealand.

Rodrigo de Oliveira and Nuria Oliver. 2008. TripleBeat: Enhancing exercise performance with persuasion. In *Proceedings of 10th International Conference, on Mobile Human-Computer Interaction*, pages 255–264, Amsterdam, the Netherlands. ACM.

Nuria Oliver and Fernando Flores-Mangas. 2006. MPTrain: A mobile, music and physiology-based personal trainer. In *Proceedings of 8th International Conference, on Mobile Human-Computer Interaction*, pages 21–28, Espoo, Finland. ACM.

Markku Turunen, Jaakko Hakulinen, Kari-Jouko Räihä, Esa-Pekka Salonen, Anssi Kainulainen, and Perttu Prusi. 2005. An architecture and applications for speech-based accessibility systems. *IBM Systems Journal*, 44(3):485–504.

Yorick Wilks. 2007. Is there progress on talking sensibly to machines? *Science*, 318(9):927–928.

[1]As described in "Loquendo embedded technologies: Text to speech and automatic speech recognition." `www.loquendo.com/en/brochure/Embedded.pdf`

Author Index